Mr Michael Rush
Eli and Edythe Broad Art Museum
Michigan State University
547 East Circle Drive
East Lansing, MI 48824

25 August 2014

Dear Mr Rush,

700 Artists' Processes, Maxime Chanson ("Book")

Please allow me to introduce myself. I am a French contemporary artist writing in regards to my latest book, **700 Artists' Processes**, which is both an artists' book and a contemporary art analysis tool.

Following the original French version of the Book in 2011, *600 démarches d'artistes,* the Book has been updated and translated into English. The official Book launch and signing was held in October 2013 at Centre Pompidou.

Several artists featured in the Book have had exhibitions within the Broad Art Museum. As such, I am glad to offer you the enclosed Book.

You will also find enclosed (i) a copy of the description which my publisher uses for the listings; and (ii) a biography.

I would be grateful if you could confirm receipt of the enclosed at mc@atelier-maximechanson.com.

Do not hesitate to contact me should you need any further information.

Yours sincerely,

Maxime Chanson

700 Artists' Processes is an artists' book which follows in the wake of the topographical charts favoured by George Maciunas and conceptual artists such as Dan Graham or Hanne Darboven. It is also a suitable tool for all artists and actors in the artworld.

Since the late 1980s, art cannot be thought of in terms of artistic movements. The innovative typology proposed by 700 Artists' Processes provides an overview of contemporary art from 1987 to 2011. This book presents a synthesis, in tabular form, of the artistic processes of approximately 700 international artists ranging from Adel Abdessemed to Heimo Zobernig.

The core area of investigation here is 'the artistic process'. This is defined as the combined action between a Motor (what drives an artist to create) and a Means (the modus operandi the artist employs).

The model developed in this book offers a general map of the concerns driving the most prominent contemporary artists and the processes through which these concerns translate into works of art. The reader will then be able to use this basis to further investigate what makes an artistic process original.

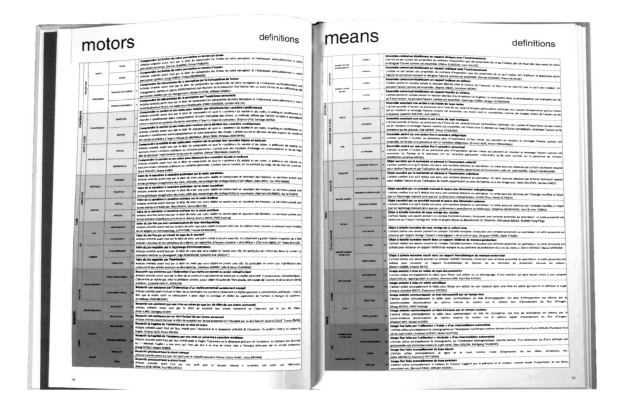

700 Artists' Processes, Book Extract

Maxime Chanson is a French contemporary artist. Born in 1983, he lives and works in Paris.

A graduate of the École Nationale Supérieure des Beaux Arts, Paris, Chanson has developed an analytical practice driven towards making explicit the vision of the actors of the artworld: artists, curators, art centres, museums, collectors, galleries, art fairs, exhibitions. His work questions the limit between art, psychology and social sciences. It takes the form of paintings, sculptures, books, performances and *in situ* installations. The artist's latest creation is a theory about the mechanism of artistic creation. In his book *700 Artists' processes*, Maxime Chanson presents the result of his study, characterising in terms of *Motors* and *Means,* the practice of the major contemporary artists.

Chanson is regularly invited to present his theory through art performances and deliver live analyses of contemporary artists participating in current exhibitions. He is also commissioned to analyse collections and exhibitions and present the result of his analyses by creating artworks some consider to be "portraits" (see example below, portrait of the Palais de Tokyo in 2013).

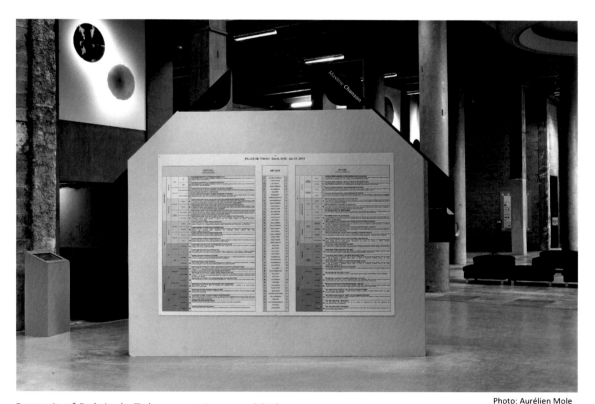

Photo: Aurélien Mole

Portrait of Palais de Tokyo as at January 2013
Information panel mounted on a wall designed by Matali Crasset, exhibited at:
L'art, mode d'emploi, Palais de Tokyo, solo show, 2013

Bonnefantenmuseum, 2013
Tables de la Loi, lacquered brass chemically engraved

700

artists' processes

contents

preface

This publication is the culmination of a unique project, carried out with a rare degree of tenacity. Spurred by the perfectly legitimate need of a young artist to define his own practice, Maxime Chanson embarked on an ambitious project, analyzing the practice of nearly seven hundred of his peers. Working with a precise set of criteria for the initial selection of artists (presented in detail in the following sections), Maxime Chanson then proceeded to methodically process each individual case, attributing generic expressions which allowed him to identify each artist's work process.

The keyword here, *process,* successfully suggests the type of action and progress that both fuels and structures the creative course — a complex phenomenon Maxime Chanson presents as the necessary alliance or combined action between a "Motor" and a "Means".

The various charts presented in this book are the fruit of a gradual and meticulous gestation; they organize and synthesize a substantial amount of data and ultimately offer a wealth of insight. If we view these charts as a whole, what emerges is a map of the contemporary artistic landscape. Indeed, the method Maxime Chanson establishes here provides an effective tool for deciphering the myriad tendencies and orientations that coexist within current creation. It serves to highlight recurrent concerns, to identify some of the key ideas and procedures that fuel both artistic production as such and its related aesthetic stakes.

In this way, the results that emerge from this in-depth inquiry support the oft-made characterization of contemporary art as a heteroclite and protean sphere, while also providing some extremely useful points of reference to help find critical bearings amid the haze. Although creation in the contemporary moment can no longer be sweepingly labeled with such and such movement, trend, or other "ism", it nonetheless continues to be articulated around major themes and shared queries that Maxime Chanson sets out to analyze.

If we consider this book at closer range, what emerges between the lines is a portrait of the artist himself. Through a mirror effect, the reflexive character of the book allows us to perceive the motivations and obsessions of its author — and surely the last chart in the book (which borrows formulas from cognitive psychology) also provides one of the keys for understanding Maxime Chanson's own stance. Bearing in mind the initial motive behind the study, it would be tempting to submit Maxime Chanson's project to its own interpretation grid. The "Motor" one would readily single out is the following: "Understanding society and its codes in order to show their conditioning nature through derision", combined with a "Contextual set that establishes a playful relationship with the visitor" as its "Means". Based on this generic definition, the classification system seems to place Maxime Chanson in good company, locating him alongside Claude Closky and Julien Prévieux, among others — artists who are also familiar with the programmatic exercise and diagrammatic data processing.

If we wanted to take this comparative game further, other more historical associations come to mind. Let's consider, for instance, the dozens of topographical charts on art George Maciunas produced between 1953 and 1973 — a colossal project, carried out in parallel with his famous series of diagrams on the historical development of Fluxus[1]. Yet *700 Artists' Processes* does not strive towards the same kind of totalizing utopia. Further, the project displays myriad similarities with some of the major principles of conceptual art: its investigation into the nature of art, its dematerialization of the artwork to privilege language, its "aesthetic of administration"[2] abounding with quantitative data, lists and all manner of systems (Dan Graham, Hanne Darboven, etc.). Georges Perec, for his part, asked in a posthumously published collection of short stories, *Penser/Classer* (Think/Classify): "How could one classify the following verbs: arrange, catalogue, classify, cut up, divide, enumerate, gather, grade, group, list, number, order, organize, sort?"[3] Maxime Chanson's work certainly keeps alive that zesty mixture of the serious and the absurd.

---

[1] See Astrit Schmidt-Burkhardt, *George Maciunas' Learning Machines. From Art History to a Chronology of Fluxus*, Vienna/New York: Springer Verlag, 2011.

[2] Benjamin H. D. Buchloh, "Conceptual Art 1962-1969: From the Aesthetic of Administration to the Critique of Institutions", *October*, Vol. 55, Winter 1990, pp. 105-143.

[3] Georges Perec, "Think/Classify" in *Species of Spaces and Other Pieces*, London: Penguin, 1997, p. 186.

He shares with the Oulipian writer a common reflection on order and categorization which, far from merely succumbing to a fascination for classification, serves, rather, to underscore the vain and illusionary dimension of all attempts to identify universal laws governing phenomena. The taxonomic vertigo that Perec discusses precisely matches the feeling the reader may experience on encountering the pages crammed with classifications compiled herein.

The reader's puzzlement will no doubt be coupled with a sense of uncertainty regarding the actual nature of this book. What is the status of a project such as this? How are we to apprehend the book-object that accompanies it? While Maxime Chanson's approach plays on ambiguities, shifting constantly between playfulness and analysis, subjectivity and objectivity, it is the actual product of his study that ultimately maintains an ambivalent identity, defying all attempts at categorization.

Prima facie, the series of charts and lists in Maxime Chanson's book are not dissimilar to the ranking lists which often feature in the specialized press, establishing the markers of celebrity and value so prized by the art market. Unless, that is, the book's methodical rigor, its strict neutrality and impersonal coldness, its hermetic appearance and general structure ultimately bring it more directly in line with an academic dissertation or a scientific report.

In this way, *700 Artists' Processes* will satisfy a variety of interests, depending on the reader. Some may approach it as an applied cognitive science exercise or a study in the sociology of art, while others will take it as an overview of the contemporary art scene and yet others as a didactic handbook for young artists. For Maxime Chanson, all of these various functions converge into a hybrid object that has enabled him to turn an initial uncertainty into a mode of creation — or, better still, an artistic form. Let's refer to this object as an artist's book[4]. We would then need to imagine the kind of distribution and circulation this kind of publishing object would have. For instance, in which section would it be placed in bookstores and libraries? Douglas Crimp has told us how he came across a copy of Ed Ruscha's famous book *Twenty-six Gasoline Stations* (1963) while doing some research in the New York Public Library one day: this work — historically accepted as the inaugural gesture of the artist's book genre — had been shelved in the general 'Transportation' section, amid books on automobiles and highways. The critic rightly observed that: "The fact that there is nowhere within the present system of classification a place for *Twenty-six Gasoline Stations* is an index of its radicalism with respect to established modes of thought"[5].

Ed Ruscha, who was himself very aware of the uncertain destiny awaiting his books, wrote a text in 1972 in which a fictitious character named "The Information Man" delivered an inventory (as comprehensive as it was comical) of the fate his books would meet[6]. However improbable, we can imagine that crossing paths with someone equipped with such omniscience would be the ideal, ultimate conclusion to Maxime Chanson's own process. I therefore invite his future readers to cooperate by sending him any comments or information they might have regarding their use of this book.

Alexandre Quoi

---

[4] See Anne Mœglin-Delcroix's seminal work on defining the artist's book genre in *Esthétique du livre d'artiste*, Paris: Jean-Michel Place, 1997.

[5] Douglas Crimp, *On the Museum's Ruins,* Cambridge, MA: The MIT Press, 1993, pp. 78.

[6] Ed Ruscha, in an interview with A. D. Coleman, "My Books End Up in the Trash", in *The New York Times*, August 27, 1972; reproduced in Ed Ruscha, *Leave Any Information at the Signal: Writings, Interviews, Bits, Pages*, Cambridge, MA: The MIT Press, 2004, pp. 46-50.

Introduction

My investigation arose from a sense of perplexity regarding my own art practice: I would contemplate the apparent diversity of themes, styles and techniques at work, yet I was unable to apprehend my own artistic singularity.

Although I believed it should show through in my work (and what all artists ultimately want is for their originality to be recognized), I was incapable of properly perceiving it.

As I lacked perspective on my own practice, I decided to focus my inquiry on others, studying the artistic process of over 700 contemporary artists, both French and international.

I centered my attention on identifying their artistic originality, on seeing whether I could find a consistent pattern, some permanent elements in terms of the "Motors" driving the artists and the "Means" that they employ.

The results of this study are presented here in the form of summary charts.

These results have provided answers to most of my questions, and I hope that the reader will in turn be able to use them to answer their own questions, both artistic and professional:

- Artistic, because you can use the results to compare yourself with artists who share the same concerns or use the same modus operandi as yourself, but also to quickly ascertain whether or not the territory you are occupying has been previously occupied, and in which ways.

- Professional, because in drawing up a list of the major centers in the contemporary art world — i.e., the sites that validate artists on an international or national level — the study brings together data that can help make clear-minded decisions about the direction you wish to take your career in, whether your aim is international or national.

the study

THE ARTISTS STUDIED

The study is concerned with those artists we could qualify as "recognized" artists creating contemporary art during the 1987-2011 period. In this way, the study deals with neither "influential artists", nor "good artists", nor artists "esteemed" by their milieu, but instead with artists who meet a set of explicit selection criteria meant to be as objective as possible (see Appendix p. 33 for the artist selection criteria).

The final selection featured:

- 602 artists from the international art scene;
- 148 artists from the French art scene (of which 27 are also part of the international scene).

See Appendix p. 67 for an index of the artists.

The analysis was broken down into five periods for the international art scene (1987-1999 / 2000-2002 / 2003-2005 / 2006-2008 / 2009-2011), and a single period for the French art scene (1987-2011).

THE MATERIAL STUDIED

Artists were selected on the basis of the solo exhibitions featured on their "official" résumé.

In order to study an artist's process, the following elements were taken into account: artworks, statements and writings by the artist and, in the last resort, third-party writings (gallery press releases, monographs devoted to the artist, etc.).

THE STUDY ITSELF

The study consisted in analyzing the data collected on each artist in order to identify any consistent elements, in terms of both core concerns and modi operandi.

AN ART PROCESS = A MOTOR + A MEANS

What quickly emerged from the study was that artistic processes could be grouped into families of concerns (the **Motors**) and families of modi operandi (the **Means**). An artistic process is thus understood as the combination of a specific Motor and a specific Means. One can differentiate between two artists sharing the same Motor-Means combination by attending to their artistic singularity, but this reflects a more in-depth level of analysis than that pursued in the present study.

THE MOTOR

Artists are driven by a Motor — the Motor is what actually prompts them to create. It emerges prior to the creative process as such and stems from the artist's deep-seated convictions. It is never called into question. We can draw a parallel here with certain theories in the field of cognitive psychology (see p. 62). Artists maintain the same Motor throughout their life although they may appear to shift between Motors in the early stages of their career.

The Motor is the underlying priority need the artist is trying to satisfy. An artist's Motor is characterized by one of the following fundamental needs:

- Understanding: artists belonging to this group are primarily driven by a need to understand and are mainly interested in themes tied to perception or the "system" (society and its codes, politics);
- Doing: artists belonging to this group are primarily driven by a need to shape or construct an alternative "reality". They alter or create a reality mainly through narration and play;
- Experiencing: artists belonging to this group are primarily driven by a need to experience or feel and are mainly interested in themes pertaining to the body and personal identity.

Each fundamental need is broken down into three successive aggregation levels, ultimately providing a list of twenty-four different Motors. The chart presenting the four levels is the "Motor Chart" (see p. 16). Each column presents a different aggregation level, going from the most fundamental, on the left (one of the three priority needs), to the most specific, on the right (the Motor itself).

Each of the twenty-four Motors (numbered from 1 to 24 to simplify their referencing in this book) is given both a brief definition (sentences in bold font, reiterating the terms of the four aggregation levels) and an expanded definition. What becomes apparent is that the Motor notion not only encapsulates what drives an artist's quest but also the way they pursue it, i.e., their angle of attack.

THE MEANS

Driven by their Motor, individual artists then create works that may seem very diverse in form (ranging from video to performance, photography, painting, installation, etc.). However, at a stage preceding the choice of medium, one observes a certain consistency in the artist's modus operandi. This level is referred to as the "Means". An artist's Means may shift in the early stages of a career but will ultimately become stable. In a similar fashion to the descriptions provided for the Motors, the Means chart gives a brief description (sentence in bold font) and an expanded description of each of the twenty-four Means (see p. 17).

motors / means

motors

UNDERSTANDING	PERCEPTION	LIMITS	TIME	1	**Understanding the limits of our perception in terms of time** Artists primarily driven by a desire to understand the limits of our perception, paying particular attention to our perception of time. (Darren ALMOND, Simon STARLING)
			SPACE	2	**Understanding the limits of our perception in terms of space** Artists primarily driven by a desire to understand the limits of our perception, paying particular attention to our perception of space. (Jorge PARDO, Tobias REHBERGER)
		MECHANISMS	FORMAT TRANSPOSITION	3	**Understanding the mechanisms of perception through format transposition** Artists primarily driven by a desire to understand the mechanisms of our perception, paying particular attention to the changes (i.e., lost or added data) that result from translating elements from one format to another and to the variations in perception occasioned by these changes. (Wade GUYTON, Wilhelm SASNAL)
			SENSORY EXPERIENCE	4	**Understanding the mechanisms of perception through sensory experience** Artists primarily driven by a desire to understand the mechanisms of our perception, paying particular attention to the physical sensations that arise through an unusual experience. (Olafur ELIASSON, Carsten HÖLLER)
	SOCIETY/CODES	CONDITIONING	MIMESIS	5	**Understanding society and its codes in order to show their conditioning nature through mimesis** Artists primarily driven by a desire to understand the ways in which the "system" (society and its codes, politics) conditions or seeks to condition our behavior and our appraisal of things. The method the artist employs consists in reproducing certain aspects of the system in order to submit them to the critical scrutiny of the spectator. (Fabrice GYGI, Santiago SIERRA)
			DERISION	6	**Understanding society and its codes in order to show their conditioning nature through derision** Artists primarily driven by a desire to understand the ways in which the "system" (society and its codes, politics) conditions or seeks to condition our behavior and our appraisal of things. The artist derides certain aspects of the system in order to submit them to the critical scrutiny of the spectator. (Mark DION, Christian JANKOWSKI)
		UNJUST/ EXCLUSIONARY	ACTS OF SHARING	7	**Understanding society and its codes in order to show their unjust and exclusionary nature through acts of sharing** Artists primarily driven by a desire to understand the ways in which the "system" (society and its codes, politics) is unjust or exclusionary towards certain practices or persons. The artist creates situations for exchange, communication and sharing in order to implicitly denounce the system's shortcomings. (Rirkrit TIRAVANIJA, MAREPE)
			DENUNCIATION	8	**Understanding society and its codes in order to denounce their unjust and exclusionary nature** Artists primarily driven by a desire to understand the ways in which the "system" (society and its codes, politics) is unjust or exclusionary towards certain practices or persons. The artist critically highlights the system's shortcomings. (Kara WALKER, Ghada AMER)
DOING	NARRATION	GROTESQUE	PARODIC	9	**Creating grotesque narratives using the parodic mode** Artists primarily driven by a desire to create an alternative reality by constructing and telling narratives. The storytelling takes on a grotesque and parodic form (exaggerating the protagonists' features, attitudes, body type). (John BOCK, Tom FRIEDMAN)
			DISQUIETING	10	**Creating grotesque narratives using the disquieting mode** Artists primarily driven by a desire to create an alternative reality by constructing and telling narratives. The storytelling takes on a grotesque and disquieting quality (exaggerating the protagonists' features, attitudes, body type). (Nathalie DJURBERG, Kai ALTHOFF)
		DREAMLIKE	DRAMATIC	11	**Creating dreamlike narratives using the dramatic mode** Artists primarily driven by a desire to create an alternative reality by constructing and telling narratives. The storytelling takes on a dreamlike and dramatic quality. (Neo RAUCH, Daniel RICHTER)
			POETIC	12	**Creating dreamlike narratives using the poetic mode** Artists primarily driven by a desire to create an alternative reality by constructing and telling narratives. The storytelling takes on a dreamlike and poetic quality, akin to reverie. (Enrico DAVID, YANG Fudong)
	PLAY	LIGHT-HEARTED	MARKETING	13	**Creating light-hearted play using marketing-type forms of communication** Artists primarily driven by a desire to create an alternative reality by playing with it. They create works modeled on marketing strategies. (Jeff KOONS, Takashi MURAKAMI)
			DIY	14	**Creating light-hearted play through DIY-type work** Artists primarily driven by a desire to create an alternative reality by playing with it. They endeavor to maintain an imperfect "homemade" quality in their creative process, as opposed to a "no flaws" industrial finish. (Christian MARCLAY, Robin RHODE)
		MORBID	ENVIRONMENTS	15	**Creating morbid play by shaping environments** Artists primarily driven by a desire to create an alternative reality by playing with it. In particular by creating sites or worlds presenting a morbid or unsettling quality. (Ugo RONDINONE, ELMGREEN & DRAGSET)
			HYBRIDIZATION	16	**Creating morbid play through hybridization** Artists primarily driven by a desire to create an alternative reality by playing with it. In particular by creating morbid or unsettling creatures and entities through hybridization. (Matthew BARNEY, Jake & Dinos CHAPMAN)
EXPERIENCING	SELF	PERSONAL MYTH	METAPHYSICAL PROJECT	17	**Experiencing one's existence by creating a personal myth endowed with a metaphysical project** Artists primarily driven by a desire to construct an identity for themselves by developing a personal myth imbued with metaphysical overtones — i.e., a mythology characterized, according to the globally accepted definition, as "the quest for absolute being, the causes of the universe and the nature of matter". (Jonathan MEESE, ABSALON)
			SOCIALLY ENGAGED	18	**Experiencing one's existence by creating a socially engaged personal myth** Artists primarily driven by a desire to construct an identity for themselves by developing a personal myth imbued with political overtones — i.e., the myth they construct takes politics as its object and reveals the artist's aspirations to change the system. (Ai Weiwei, Shirin NESHAT)
		PERSONAL DRAMA	ROLE-PLAY	19	**Experiencing one's existence via a role-play-type staging of one's personal drama** Artists primarily driven by a desire to experience their existential drama — exploring it via role-play. (Peter LAND, Georgina STARR)
			FACTUAL NARRATIVE	20	**Experiencing one's existence via a factual narrative of one's personal drama** Artists primarily driven by a desire to experience their existential drama — exploring it via factual narrative. (Sophie CALLE, Tracey EMIN)
	BODY	FRAGILITY	STAGING	21	**Experiencing the fragility of existence through its staging** Artists primarily driven by their interest in the ephemeral and the unstable dimension of existence. They seek to stage the fragile. (Francis ALŸS, Erwin WURM)
			AURATIC PRESENCE	22	**Experiencing the fragility of existence through auratic presentification** Artists primarily driven by their interest in the fragile, the ephemeral and the unstable dimension of existence. They make work in which the "fragile element" possesses an aura that does not derive from its staging but from the energy mediated by its sheer presence. (Doug AITKEN, Robert GOBER)
		PLEASURE	SENSUALITY	23	**Physically experiencing sensual pleasure** Artists primarily driven by their taste for sensual and carnal experiences. (Gary HUME, Cecily BROWN)
			TRASHINESS	24	**Physically experiencing trashy pleasure** Artists primarily driven by their taste for intense trashy or fetishistic experiences. (Monica BONVINCINI, Paul MCCARTHY)

means   definitions

			#	Definition
SET	CONTEXTUAL	WORK-ENVIRONMENT RELATIONSHIP	CLINICAL	1	**Contextual set that establishes a clinical relationship with the environment** The artist draws on the properties of the exhibition context and the properties of their actual creation in equal measure in order to intertwine the two and designate the work as this set. (Olafur ELIASSON, Liam GILLICK)
			DREAMLIKE	2	**Contextual set that establishes a dreamlike relationship with the environment** The artist draws on the properties of the exhibition context and the properties of their actual creation in equal measure in order to erase the distinction between the two and designate the work as this set. (Darren ALMOND, Pierre HUYGHE)
		WORK-VISITOR RELATIONSHIP	PLAYFUL	3	**Contextual set that establishes a playful relationship with the visitor** The artist takes into account, in equal measure, the reaction they hope to elicit from visitors (in this case: amusement, laughter, etc.) and what they must create, and apprehends the work as this set. (Martin CREED, Jonathan MONK)
			HOSTILE	4	**Contextual set that establishes a hostile relationship with the visitor** The artist takes into account, in equal measure, the reaction they hope to elicit from visitors (in this case: discomfort or constrained movement, for instance) and what they must create, and apprehends the work as this set. (Santiago SIERRA, Gregor SCHNEIDER)
	ASSOCIATING AN ACTION	TRACES	REMAINS	5	**Set that associates an action with its remains-type traces** The artist attributes equal importance to the action, the process, or one of their specific features (attitude, etc.) and to the traces which result from them, and apprehends the work as this set. Here, the traces are considered as simple remains of the action or process. (Joachim KOESTER, Josh SMITH)
			ICONIC	6	**Set that associates an action with its icon-type traces** The artist attributes equal importance to the action, the process, or one of their specific features (attitude, etc.) and to the traces which result from them, and apprehends the work as this set. Here, the traces are elevated to the status of icons, symbolizing or embodying the preceding action or process. (Vik MUNIZ, Simon STARLING)
		LIVE	ALLEGORY	7	**Set centered around a live, allegorical action** The artist attributes more importance to the action or process than to the traces that may result from them and apprehends the work as this set. Here, the action and process are of an allegorical nature. (Francis ALŸS, Rirkrit TIRAVANIJA)
			THE INDIVIDUAL	8	**Set centered around a live, personal action** The artist attributes more importance to the action or process than to the traces that may result from them and apprehends the work as this set. Here, the action and process are of a personal nature, i.e., centered around the physical involvement of the artist. (KIMSOOJA, Jonathan MEESE)
OBJECT	SACRALIZED	TECHNICAL CHARACTER	COLLECTIVE UNCONSCIOUS	9	**Object sacralized by its technical character and directed towards the collective unconscious** The artist endows what they make with an aura, a certain distance vis-à-vis the spectator. Here, the aura is achieved through the high level of technical prowess required to make the work and by the use of motifs and symbols pertaining to the collective unconscious. (Jeff KOONS, Takashi MURAKAMI)
			INDIVIDUAL UNCONSCIOUS	10	**Object sacralized by its technical character and directed towards the individual unconscious** The artist endows what they make with an aura, a certain distance vis-à-vis the spectator. Here, the aura is achieved through the high level of technical prowess required to make the work and by the use of motifs pertaining to the life experience or imaginary of the artist. (Wim DELVOYE, Damien HIRST)
		MANUAL PROCESS	METAPHYSICAL DIMENSION	11	**Object sacralized through a manual process, presenting a metaphysical dimension** The artist endows what they make with an aura, a certain distance vis-à-vis the spectator. Here, the aura is created through the energy infused into the object (through handcrafting) and through its metaphysical dimension. (CHEN Zhen, David ALTMEJD)
			PAGAN DIMENSION	12	**Object sacralized through a manual process, presenting a pagan dimension** The artist endows what they make with an aura, a certain distance vis-à-vis the spectator. Here, the aura is achieved through the energy infused into the object (through handcrafting) and through its everyday or folkloric dimension. (Stephan BALKENHOL, Gert & Uwe TOBIAS)
	HUMAN SCALE	VESTIGE	UTOPIAS	13	**Human-scale, 'vestige of the utopias'-type object** The artist creates a work that takes human scale into account, establishing a certain proximity with the spectator. Here, the proximity is reinforced by the vestigial aspect of Man's disappointed dreams and abandonned projects. (Miroslaw BALKA, HUANG Yong Ping)
			POP CULTURE	14	**Human-scale, 'vestige of pop culture'-type object** The artist creates a work that takes human scale into account, establishing a certain proximity with the spectator. Here, the proximity is achieved through the vestigial, 'nostalgic' aspect of pop culture. (Grayson PERRY, Keith TYSON)
		THREAT/ PROTECTION RELATION	DRAMATIC	15	**Human-scale object inscribed in a dramatic threat/protection relation** The artist creates a work that takes human scale into account, establishing a certain proximity with the spectator. Here, the proximity is used to establish a dramatic relation based on threat or, conversely, protection vis-à-vis the visitor. (Shirin NESHAT, Mona HATOUM)
			KINESTHETIC	16	**Human-scale object inscribed in a kinesthetic threat/protection relation** The artist creates a work that takes human scale into account, establishing a certain proximity with the spectator. Here, the proximity is used to establish a kinesthetic relation based on threat or, conversely, protection vis-à-vis the visitor. (Robert GOBER, Ernesto NETO)
IMAGE	MOVING	MISE-EN-SCENE	DOCUMENTARY-STYLE	17	**Moving image with documentary-style mise-en-scene** The artist mainly uses video to shoot an action or testimony in a manner suggesting the objectivity of the gaze directing the camera. (Aernout MIK, Eija-Liisa AHTILA)
			PARODIC	18	**Moving image with parodic mise-en-scene** The artist mainly uses video to shoot an action or situation staged to deride its subject. (Candice BREITZ, Francesco VEZZOLI)
		STATE	SLOW TEMPO	19	**Moving image conveying an introspective state through a slow tempo** The artist mainly uses video to convey an introspective state. This introspective state is achieved through the (unconscious) synchronization of the visitor's inner rhythm and the slow flow of images. (Doug AITKEN, YANG Fudong)
			RAPID TEMPO	20	**Moving image conveying an intoxicated state through a rapid tempo** The artist mainly uses video to convey a state of stimulation. This state of stimulation is achieved through the (unconscious) synchronization of the visitor's inner rhythm and the rapid flow of images. (Pipilotti RIST, Michel AUDER)
	STILL	AUTOMATED INTERMEDIARY	COLD USE	21	**Still image produced through the "cold" use of an automated intermediary** The artist mainly uses photography or digital printing to witness a process or analytical attitude vis-à-vis the subject. (Andreas GURSKY, Wade GUYTON)
			VISCERAL USE	22	**Still image produced through the "visceral" use of an automated intermediary** The artist mainly uses photography or instant photography to witness a process or an impulsive or instinctive attitude vis-à-vis the subject. (Nan GOLDIN, Wolfgang TILLMANS)
		HAND-CRAFTED	DRAWING	23	**Still, handcrafted image — drawing type** The artist mainly uses the drawn line as the medium for expressing their ideas and sensations, etc. (Julie MEHRETU, Raymond PETTIBON)
			PAINTING	24	**Still, handcrafted image — painting type** The artist mainly uses the space suggested by the paint and color as the medium for expressing their ideas and sensations, etc. (Bernard FRIZE, Wilhelm SASNAL)

means: supplementary definition

SET: Any Means that cannot be reduced to either Image or Object Means.

– **CONTEXTUAL SET**:

Any Set-type Means, conceived from the outset of the creative process in terms of the relationship with the visitor or the exhibition context.

IMAGE: A two-dimensional presentation of autonomous visual data (not conceived in terms of the data's relationship to their surrounding context). An image may include three-dimensional or textual elements as long as their role is not central to the piece. In the opposite case, the previously overlooked support would emerge in its primary function: as the physical support of the three-dimensional or textual elements, thus giving the whole the status of "Object Means" or "Set Means".

Note: In general, when the characteristics of the support are manifest, one will most often be dealing with an Object- or Set-type Means rather than an Image-type Means (e.g., a monochrome painting or a painting featuring repetitive motifs or schemes, etc.).

– **STILL, HANDCRAFTED IMAGE — DRAWING TYPE**:

In this type of image, the line plays a crucial role through its descriptive, figurative qualities and/or through its intrinsic graphic qualities. The line provides the point of entry into the space of a drawing. Photomontage, a medium which is graphical above all, also falls under this category.

– **STILL, HANDCRAFTED IMAGE — PAINTING TYPE**:

An image primarily characterized by the sensory qualities of the matter and not by its graphic dimension (the line) or its descriptive dimension. Unlike in a drawing, where the line provides the point of entry, with a painting, one enters the space through the matter and through color. A drawing made with paint is not necessarily a painting. Conversely, a painting featuring numerous lines is not necessarily a drawing.

– **STILL IMAGE PRODUCED THROUGH THE USE OF AN AUTOMATED INTERMEDIARY**:

A specific category of the Image Means in which the artist uses an automated intermediary such as a camera, a printing device, etc. Here, the artist acts as the "trigger" in a process of unfolding chained actions.

OBJECT: An object in the classic sense of the word, i.e., an individualized thing with finite contours, endowed with intrinsic characteristics independent from its environment.

artist
classification charts

					1987-1999	2000-2002
UNDERSTANDING	PERCEPTION	LIMITS	TIME	1	T. DEAN / P. HUYGHE / J. KOESTER / S. LOCKHART	D. ALMOND / D. CLAERBOUT / T. DEAN / L. HEMPEL / P. HUYGHE / J. KOESTER / M. LEWIS / S. LOCKHART / S. STARLING
			SPACE	2	G. FÖRG / A. GURSKY / C. HÖFER / C. IGLESIAS / R. KHEDOORI / J. PARDO / T. REHBERGER / A. TAYLOR	F. ACKERMANN / M. BARTOLINI / A. BULLOCH / P. CABRITA REIS / M. FRANÇOIS / A. GURSKY / C. HÖFER / HUBBARD & BIRCHLER / C. IGLESIAS / R. KHEDOORI / W. J. LIM / J. PARDO / T. REHBERGER
		MECHANISMS	FORMAT TRANSPOSITION	3	J. COLEMAN / T. DEMAND / H.-P. FELDMANN / I. H. FINLAY / C. FLOYER / K. FRITSCH / M. HONERT / R. HORN / B. LAVIER / S. PIPPIN / T. RUFF / T. STRUTH / X. VEILHAN / J. WELLING / WILCOX T. J. / C. WILLIAMS / C. WYN EVANS	J. COLEMAN / M. COLLISHAW / DE ROOIJ (DE RIJKE & DE ROOIJ <2006) / T. DEMAND / C. FLOYER / E. HAVEKOST / C. PARKER / P. PFEIFFER / R. PHILLIPS / B. PIFFARETTI / S. PIPPIN / T. RUFF / T. STRUTH / P. UKLANSKI / X. VEILHAN / WILCOX T. J. / C. WILLIAMS / C. WYN EVANS
			SENSORY EXPERIENCE	4	O. ELIASSON / J. LASKER / B. LE VA / J. STOCKHOLDER	J. CARDIFF / J. DODGE / O. ELIASSON / T. FERNÁNDEZ / S. FINCH / B. FRIZE / C. HÖLLER / J. LASKER / J. STOCKHOLDER
	SOCIETY/CODES	CONDITIONING	MIMESIS	5	CLEGG & GUTTMANN / A. DENNIS / L. GILLICK / P. HALLEY / R. HAWKINS / S. LEVINE / K. LUM / A. MCCOLLUM / S. MORRIS / M. PERNICE / G. ROCKENSCHAUB / J. SCHER / H. STEINBACH / A. ZITTEL / H. ZOBERNIG	K. ATAMAN / L. GILLICK / R. HAWKINS / S. LEVINE / K. LUM / S. MORRIS / S. SIERRA / WANG DU / A. ZITTEL
			DERISION	6	M. DION / G. HEROLD / L. LAWLER / R. PETTIBON / S. PRINA / R. TROCKEL / F. WEST	M. DION / S. DURANT / J. HOROWITZ / C. JANKOWSKI / A. LARSSON / L. LAWLER / R. PETTIBON / S. PRINA / R. TROCKEL
		UNJUST/ EXCLUSIONARY	ACTS OF SHARING	7	CHEN ZHEN / F. GONZALEZ-TORRES / HUANG YONG PING / A. JAAR / T. ROLLINS & K.O.S / R. TIRAVANIJA / XU BING	HUANG YONG PING / A. JAAR / KIMSOOJA / R. NEUESCHWANDER / R. TIRAVANIJA
			DENUNCIATION	8	W. DOHERTY / S. DOUGLAS / R. GREEN / D. HAMMONS / Z. LEONARD / T. MOFFATT / C. NOLAND / A. PIPER / D. THATER	G. AMER / W. DOHERTY / S. DOUGLAS / M. FARRELL / J-A. HERNÁNDEZ-DÍEZ / I. JULIEN / Z. LEONARD / T. MOFFATT / D. PETERMAN / Y. SHONIBARE / D. THATER / B. TOGUO / Ka. WALKER / J. & L. WILSON
DOING	NARRATION	GROTESQUE	PARODIC	9	T. FRIEDMAN	J. BOCK / T. FRIEDMAN / B. MCGEE / M. OCAMPO
			DISQUIETING	10	J. BEDIA / A. SCHULZE	J. BEDIA / B. MELGAARD / L. SCHNITGER
		DREAMLIKE	DRAMATIC	11		A. GASKELL / W. KENTRIDGE / N. RAUCH / G. TODERI
			POETIC	12	B. BLOOM / P. DOIG / K. KILIMNIK / J.-M. OTHONIEL / A. STRBA	V. DAWSON / P. DOIG / K. KILIMNIK / M. PLESSEN / D. ROTH / A. STRBA
	PLAY	LIGHT-HEARTED	MARKETING	13	W. DELVOYE / J. KOONS / T. MURAKAMI / J. RHOADES	W. DELVOYE / U. FISCHER / S. FLEURY / J. KOONS / T. MURAKAMI / J. RHOADES
			DIY	14	U. KRISANAMIS / D. MULLER / A. OEHLEN / L. PITTMAN / R. SIGNER / R. THERRIEN	L. CRAFT / U. KRISANAMIS / LOS CARPINTEROS / M. MAJERUS / C. MARCLAY / V. MUNIZ / R. PRUITT / J. SCANLAN
		MORBID	ENVIRONMENTS	15	M. CATTELAN / D. HIRST / P. PARRENO	M. CATTELAN / ELMGREEN & DRAGSET / C. LÉVÊQUE / P. PARRENO / U. RONDINONE / M. SCHINWALD
			HYBRIDIZATION	16	M. BARNEY / J. & D. CHAPMAN / K. EDMIER / E. GALLAGHER / T. SCHÜTTE / B. X BALL	C. AMORALES / M. BARNEY / E. GALLAGHER / M. JOO / B. MARTIN / T. SCHÜTTE / A. VAREJÃO
EXPERIENCING	SELF	PERSONAL MYTH	METAPHYSICAL PROJECT	17	ABSALON / J. ANTONI / ATELIER VAN LIESHOUT / J. FABRE / T. HIRSCHHORN / F. HYBER / L. LAMBRI / T. MIYAJIMA / M. MORI / K. SMITH / J. STERBAK	R. ACKERMANN / ATELIER VAN LIESHOUT / DO-HO SUH / T. HIRSCHHORN / Z. HUAN / F. HYBER / M. MANDERS / T. MIYAJIMA / M. MORI / K. SMITH
			SOCIALLY ENGAGED	18	I. APPLEBROOG / K. GEERS / S. NESHAT / C. SAMBA	P. ALTHAMER / K. GEERS / M. GUILLEMINOT / S. NESHAT
		PERSONAL DRAMA	ROLE-PLAY	19	D. GORDON / R. GRAHAM / I. & E. KABAKOV / M. KELLEY / M. KIPPENBERGER / P. LAND / J. MILLER / Y. MORIMURA / J. MUÑOZ / J. OPIE / G. STARR / G. WEARING	F. ALŸS / C. BREITZ / O. BREUNING / P. CHANG / J. DUNNING / D. GORDON / R. GRAHAM / I. & E. KABAKOV / M. KELLEY / P. LAND / M. MARSHALL / Y. MORIMURA / J. MUÑOZ / Y. NARA / J. OPIE / J. SHAW / L. SIMPSON / V. TANDBERG / G. WEARING
			FACTUAL NARRATIVE	20	S. CALLE / D. DIAO / T. EMIN / S. MCQUEEN / N. SOLAKOV	E-L. AHTILA / S. CALLE / M. CREED / T. EMIN / S. MCQUEEN / J. MONK
	BODY		STAGING	21	D. BAECHLER / C. BORLAND / L. CLARK / G. CREWDSON / P.-L. DICORCIA / B. MIKHAILOV / J. PIERSON / M. QUINN / A. SEKULA / S. TAYLOR-WOOD / J. WALL	R. BALLEN / V. BEECROFT / C. BORLAND / P.-L. DICORCIA / MUNTEAN & ROSENBLUM / J. ONOFRE / J. PIERSON / M. QUINN / A. SALA / D. SHRIGLEY / S. TAYLOR-WOOD / J. WALL / E. WURM
		FRAGILITY	AURATIC PRESENCE	22	M. AUDER / M. BALKA / S. BALKENHOL / R. BLECKNER / J.-M. BUSTAMANTE / J. CASEBERE / M. DUMAS / A. GALLACCIO / I. GENZKEN / R. GOBER / M. HATOUM / G. HILL / S. HOUSHIARY / G. KUITCA / G. OROZCO / E. PEYTON / J. PLENSA / M. PURYEAR / C. RAY / S. SAMORE / J. SARMENTO / B. STREULI / H. SUGIMOTO / P. TAAFFE / W. TILLMANS / P. TOSANI / L. TUYMANS / A. UGLOW / R. WHITEREAD / C. WOOL	D. AITKEN / H. AKAKÇE / K. ASDAM / M. BALKA / S. BALKENHOL / R. BLECKNER / J.-M. BUSTAMANTE / R. DIJKSTRA / M. DUMAS / E. ESSER / A. GALLACCIO / R. GOBER / M. HATOUM / S. HOUSHIARY / LEE BUL / L. LOU / P. MORRISON / R. MUECK / G. OROZCO / E. PEYTON / C. PIENE / J. PLENSA / J. RIELLY / S. SAMORE / J. SARMENTO / B. STREULI / H. SUGIMOTO / P. TAAFFE / F. TAN / W. TILLMANS / L. TUYMANS / S. TYKKÄ / R. WHITEREAD / C. WOOL / R. WRIGHT
		PLEASURE	SENSUALITY	23	J. CURRIN / N. HIRAKAWA / G. HUME / F. RAE / P. RIST / T. SCHEIBITZ / I. VAN LAMSWEERDE / S. WILLIAMS	C. BROWN / J. CURRIN / K. GROSSE / A. HERRERA / G. HUME / E. NETO / P. RIST / T. SCHEIBITZ / S. WILLIAMS
			TRASHINESS	24	N. GOLDIN / S. LUCAS / F. MARCACCIO / P. MCCARTHY / S. PARRINO / A. SERRANO / N. TYSON	F. MARCACCIO / P. MCCARTHY / S. PARRINO / G. SCHNEIDER / A. SERRANO

means

international artists

SET / OBJECT / IMAGE	Category	Subcategory	Type	#	1987-1999	2000-2002
SET	CONTEXTUAL	WORK-ENVIRONMENT RELATIONSHIP	CLINICAL	1	CLEGG & GUTTMANN / O. ELIASSON / L. GILLICK / R. GREEN R. HORN / L. LAWLER / S. LEVINE / S. MORRIS J. PARDO / S. PIPPIN / S. PRINA / T. REHBERGER G. ROCKENSCHAUB / H. STEINBACH / H. ZOBERNIG	M. BARTOLINI / DE ROOIJ (DE RIJKE & DE ROOIJ <2006>) / O. ELIASSON / L. GILLICK L. LAWLER / S. LEVINE / S. MORRIS / J. PARDO P. PFEIFFER / S. PIPPIN / S. PRINA / T. REHBERGER
			DREAMLIKE	2	M. BARNEY / B. BLOOM / P. HUYGHE / A. JAAR I. & E. KABAKOV / M. KELLEY / K. KILIMNIK / T. MIYAJIMA P. PARRENO / J. PLENSA / G. STARR / D. THATER C. WYN EVANS	F. ACKERMANN / H. AKAKÇE / D. ALMOND / M. BARNEY J. CARDIFF / M. COLLISHAW / J. DODGE / S. FINCH P. HUYGHE / A. JAAR / I. & E. KABAKOV / M. KELLEY W. KENTRIDGE / K. KILIMNIK / C. LÉVÊQUE / W. J. LIM T. MIYAJIMA / P. PARRENO / J. PLENSA / A. SALA J. SHAW / D. THATER / Ka. WALKER / R. WRIGHT C. WYN EVANS
		WORK-VISITOR RELATIONSHIP	PLAYFUL	3	M. CATTELAN / C. FLOYER / F. GONZALEZ-TORRES / R. GRAHAM B. LAVIER / K. LUM / Y. MORIMURA / A. SCHULZE N. SOLAKOV	O. BREUNING / M. CATTELAN / M. CREED / ELMGREEN & DRAGSET U. FISCHER / S. FLEURY / C. FLOYER / R. GRAHAM C. HÖLLER / C. JANKOWSKI / K. LUM / J. MONK Y. MORIMURA / R. NEUESCHWANDER / D. SHRIGLEY / P. UKLANSKI E. WURM
			HOSTILE	4	J. & D. CHAPMAN / T. HIRSCHHORN / S. LUCAS / C. NOLAND J. RHOADES / J. SCHER / A. ZITTEL	A. BULLOCH / M. FARRELL / T. HIRSCHHORN / J. RHOADES G. SCHNEIDER / S. SIERRA / A. ZITTEL
	ASSOCIATING AN ACTION	TRACES	REMAINS	5	J. KOESTER / B. LE VA / A. TAYLOR	K. GROSSE / J. KOESTER / B. MCGEE
			ICONIC	6	S. CALLE / A. PIPER / XU BING	S. CALLE / V. MUNIZ / D. PETERMAN / S. STARLING
		LIVE	ALLEGORY	7	J. ANTONI / P. MCCARTHY / S. MCQUEEN / R. TIRAVANIJA	P. ALTHAMER / F. ALŸS / K. ASDAM / V. BEECROFT M. GUILLEMINOT / P. MCCARTHY / S. MCQUEEN / J. ONOFRE R. TIRAVANIJA
			THE INDIVIDUAL	8		J. BOCK / P. CHANG / KIMSOOJA
OBJECT	SACRALIZED	TECHNICAL CHARACTER	COLLECTIVE UNCONSCIOUS	9	J. KOONS / T. MURAKAMI / J. OPIE / X. VEILHAN	Z. HUAN / J. KOONS / T. MURAKAMI / J. OPIE X. VEILHAN
			INDIVIDUAL UNCONSCIOUS	10	W. DELVOYE / K. FRITSCH / D. GORDON / D. HIRST M. HONERT / S. HOUSHIARY / M. MORI / J.-M. OTHONIEL M. QUINN / C. RAY	W. DELVOYE / DO-HO SUH / T. FERNÁNDEZ / D. GORDON S. HOUSHIARY / M. MORI / R. MUECK / M. QUINN
		MANUAL PROCESS	METAPHYSICAL DIMENSION	11	CHEN ZHEN / A. DENNIS / G. KUITCA / J. SARMENTO J. STERBAK	J. SARMENTO
			PAGAN DIMENSION	12	S. BALKENHOL / C. BORLAND / T. EMIN / A. GALLACCIO R. KHEDOORI / U. KRISANAMIS / T. SCHÜTTE	S. BALKENHOL / C. BORLAND / T. EMIN / A. GALLACCIO R. KHEDOORI / U. KRISANAMIS / C. PARKER / D. ROTH T. SCHÜTTE
	HUMAN SCALE	VESTIGE	UTOPIAS	13	M. BALKA / J.-M. BUSTAMANTE / I. H. FINLAY / G. FÖRG G. HEROLD / HUANG YONG PING / M. KIPPENBERGER / A. MCCOLLUM G. OROZCO / S. PARRINO / M. PERNICE / M. PURYEAR T. ROLLINS & K.O.S / T. SCHEIBITZ / R. TROCKEL / A. UGLOW R. WHITEREAD	C. AMORALES / M. BALKA / J.-M. BUSTAMANTE / HUANG YONG PING LEE BUL / M. MANDERS / G. OROZCO / S. PARRINO T. SCHEIBITZ / R. TROCKEL / R. WHITEREAD
			POP CULTURE	14	D. BAECHLER / M. DION / H.-P. FELDMANN / T. FRIEDMAN I. GENZKEN / D. HAMMONS / R. HAWKINS / Z. LEONARD J. MILLER / D. MULLER / J. PIERSON / J. STOCKHOLDER WILCOX T. J. / C. WOOL	M. DION / T. FRIEDMAN / R. HAWKINS / L. HEMPEL J-A. HERNÁNDEZ-DÍEZ / J. HOROWITZ / Z. LEONARD / LOS CARPINTEROS M. MAJERUS / C. MARCLAY / J. PIERSON / R. PRUITT J. SCANLAN / J. STOCKHOLDER / WANG DU / WILCOX T. J. C. WOOL
		THREAT/ PROTECTION RELATION	DRAMATIC	15	ABSALON / ATELIER VAN LIESHOUT / J. FABRE / K. GEERS M. HATOUM / F. HYBER / J. MUÑOZ / S. NESHAT R. SIGNER / K. SMITH / B. THERRIEN / B. X BALL	ATELIER VAN LIESHOUT / S. DURANT / M. FRANÇOIS / K. GEERS M. HATOUM / F. HYBER / M. JOO / M. MARSHALL P. MORRISON / J. MUÑOZ / S. NESHAT / C. PIENE U. RONDINONE / M. SCHINWALD / L. SCHNITGER / Y. SHONIBARE K. SMITH
			KINESTHETIC	16	I. APPLEBROOG / K. EDMIER / R. GOBER / N. HIRAKAWA C. IGLESIAS / F. MARCACCIO / F. WEST	G. AMER / P. CABRITA REIS / L. CRAFT / J. DUNNING R. GOBER / C. IGLESIAS / L. LOU / F. MARCACCIO B. MARTIN / B. MELGAARD / E. NETO / B. TOGUO A. VAREJÃO
IMAGE	MOVING	MISE-EN-SCENE	DOCUMENTARY-STYLE	17	J. COLEMAN / S. DOUGLAS / S. LOCKHART / G. WEARING	E-L. AHTILA / K. ATAMAN / J. COLEMAN / S. DOUGLAS I. JULIEN / S. LOCKHART / L. SIMPSON / V. TANDBERG G. WEARING / J. & L. WILSON
			PARODIC	18	P. LAND	C. BREITZ / P. LAND
		STATE	SLOW TEMPO	19	T. DEAN / W. DOHERTY / G. HILL / S. SAMORE A. STRBA / S. TAYLOR-WOOD	D. AITKEN / D. CLAERBOUT / T. DEAN / W. DOHERTY HUBBARD & BIRCHLER / A. LARSSON / M. LEWIS / S. SAMORE A. STRBA / F. TAN / S. TAYLOR-WOOD / G. TODERI S. TYKKÄ
			RAPID TEMPO	20	M. AUDER / P. RIST	P. RIST
	STILL	AUTOMATED INTERMEDIARY	COLD USE	21	J. CASEBERE / G. CREWDSON / T. DEMAND / P.-L. DICORCIA A. GURSKY / C. HÖFER / L. LAMBRI / T. RUFF A. SEKULA / A. SERRANO / B. STREULI / T. STRUTH H. SUGIMOTO / P. TOSANI / J. WALL / J. WELLING C. WILLIAMS	T. DEMAND / P.-L. DICORCIA / R. DIJKSTRA / E. ESSER A. GURSKY / C. HÖFER / T. RUFF / A. SERRANO B. STREULI / T. STRUTH / H. SUGIMOTO / J. WALL C. WILLIAMS
			VISCERAL USE	22	L. CLARK / N. GOLDIN / B. MIKHAILOV / T. MOFFATT W. TILLMANS / I. VAN LAMSWEERDE	R. BALLEN / A. GASKELL / T. MOFFATT / W. TILLMANS
		HAND-CRAFTED	DRAWING	23	E. GALLAGHER / R. PETTIBON	E. GALLAGHER / A. HERRERA / MUNTEAN & ROSENBLUM / Y. NARA R. PETTIBON
			PAINTING	24	J. BEDIA / R. BLECKNER / J. CURRIN / D. DIAO P. DOIG / M. DUMAS / P. HALLEY / G. HUME J. LASKER / A. OEHLEN / E. PEYTON / L. PITTMAN F. RAE / C. SAMBA / P. TAAFFE / L. TUYMANS N. TYSON / S. WILLIAMS	R. ACKERMANN / J. BEDIA / R. BLECKNER / C. BROWN J. CURRIN / V. DAWSON / P. DOIG / M. DUMAS B. FRIZE / E. HAVEKOST / G. HUME / J. LASKER M. OCAMPO / E. PEYTON / R. PHILLIPS / B. PIFFARETTI M. PLESSEN / N. RAUCH / J. RIELLY / P. TAAFFE L. TUYMANS / S. WILLIAMS

motors

				#	2003-2005	2006-2008
UNDERSTANDING	PERCEPTION	LIMITS	TIME	1	D. ALMOND / M. BUCKINGHAM / T. DEAN / T. DONNELLY / P. HUYGHE / M. LEWIS / S. LOCKHART / M. OHANIAN / S. STARLING / M. STEVENSON / SU-MEI TSE	D. ALMOND / M. BUCKINGHAM / D. CLAERBOUT / T. DEAN / T. DONNELLY / L. HEMPEL / P. HUYGHE / J. KOESTER / S. LOCKHART / J. MACCHI / D. MALJKOVIĆ / M. OHANIAN / S. STARLING / M. STEVENSON / K. STRUNZ / J. WOLFSON
			SPACE	2	F. ACKERMANN / A. BULLOCH / P. CABRITA REIS / A. ERKMEN / M. FRANÇOIS / A. GURSKY / J. HEIN / HUBBARD & BIRCHLER / C. IGLESIAS / W.J. LIM / D. ORTEGA / J. PARDO / S. PREGO / T. REHBERGER	M. BARTOLINI / J. DE COCK / L. ERLICH / A. GURSKY / J. HEIN / HUBBARD & BIRCHLER / C. IGLESIAS / W.J. LIM / J. MEHRETU / R. ONDÁK / D. ORTEGA / J. PARDO / T. PUTRIH / T. REHBERGER / G. SIBONY / N. WERMERS / C. YASS
		MECHANISMS	FORMAT TRANSPOSITION	3	B. DAHLEM / DE ROOIJ (DE RIJKE & DE ROOIJ <2006) / T. DEMAND / C. FLOYER / G. GABELLONE / W. GUYTON / E. HAVEKOST / J. MCELHENY / C. PARKER / P. PFEIFFER / R. PHILLIPS / T. RUFF / W. SASNAL / P. UKLANSKI / WILCOX T.J. / C. WYN EVANS	DE ROOIJ (DE RIJKE & DE ROOIJ <2006) / T. DEMAND / O. FAST / C. FLOYER / W. GUYTON / E. HAVEKOST / A. KELM / J. MCELHENY / P. PFEIFFER / D. PFLUMM / W. SASNAL / WILCOX T. J.
			SENSORY EXPERIENCE	4	J. CARDIFF / J. DODGE / O. ELIASSON / T. FERNÁNDEZ / S. FINCH / B. FRIZE / C. HÖLLER / A.V. JANSSENS / J. LASKER / J. STOCKHOLDER	T. ABTS / J. CARDIFF / I. DO ESPERITO SANTO / J. DODGE / O. ELIASSON / S. FINCH / C. HÖLLER / J. MARTIN / J. STOCKHOLDER / P. ZIMMERMAN
	SOCIETY/CODES	CONDITIONING	MIMESIS	5	K. ATAMAN / Y. BARTANA / A. FRASER / L. GILLICK / F. GYGI / A. MIK / S. MORRIS / H. OP DE BEECK / S. SIERRA / C. SULLIVAN / F. VEZZOLI / A. ZITTEL / A. ZMIJEWSKI	K. ATAMAN / Y. BARTANA / C. BÜCHEL / G. BYRNE / J. DELLER / A. FRASER / L. GILLICK / Su. GUPTA / R. HAWKINS / A. MIK / S. MORRIS / H. OP DE BEECK / J. SMITH / R. SPAULINGS / C. SULLIVAN / SUPERFLEX / F. VEZZOLI / Ke. WALKER / WANG DU / A. ZITTEL / A. ZMIJEWSKI
			DERISION	6	A. BUBLEX / M. DION / S. DURANT / C. GARAICOA / R. HARRISON / C. JANKOWSKI / A. LARSSON / G. LIGON / L. MCKENZIE / R. PETTIBON / A. SLOMINSKI / J. WOHNSEIFER / S. XHAFA	ALLORA & CALZADILLA / P. BISMUTH / M. DION / C. FONTAINE / C. GARAICOA / R. HARRISON / C. JANKOWSKI / G. LIGON / L. MCKENZIE / G. PERRY / R. PETTIBON / S. XHAFA
		UNJUST/ EXCLUSIONARY	ACTS OF SHARING	7	HUANG YONG PING / KIMSOOJA / R. NEUESCHWANDER / R. TIRAVANIJA	ASSUME VIVID ASTRO POCUS / HUANG YONG PING / KIMSOOJA / MAREPE / R. NEUESCHWANDER / P. REYES / R. TIRAVANIJA / C. VON BONIN
			DENUNCIATION	8	G. AMER / M. BAJEVIC / A. BOWERS / W. DOHERTY / S. DOUGLAS / H. FAROCKI / J-A. HERNÁNDEZ-DÍEZ / E. JACIR / I. JULIEN / I. MANGLANO-OVALLE / J. NGUYEN-HATSUSHJBA / Y. SHONIBARE / T. SIMON / D. THATER / Ka. WALKER / J. & L. WILSON	G. AMER / ATLAS GROUP (WALID RAAD) / A. BOWERS / T. BRUGUERA / M. CUEVAS / S. DOUGLAS / H. FAROCKI / J. HANNING / J-A. HERNÁNDEZ-DÍEZ / E. JACIR / I. JULIEN / J. NGUYEN-HATSUSHJBA / D. PERJOVSCHI / Y. SHONIBARE / T. SIMON / D. THATER / Ka. WALKER / J. & L. WILSON
DOING	NARRATION	GROTESQUE	PARODIC	9	J. BOCK / S. CHETWYND / T. FRIEDMAN / B. FURNAS / B. MCGEE / K. TYSON	G. BEN-NER / J. BOCK / S. CHETWYND / B. MCGEE / K. TYSON
			DISQUIETING	10	K. ALTHOFF / B. MELGAARD / L. SCHNITGER	K. ALTHOFF / N. COOKE / N. DJURBERG / R. FEINSTEIN / R. SHAW
		DREAMLIKE	DRAMATIC	11	M. DZAMA / N. HESS / W. KENTRIDGE / N. RAUCH / D. RICHTER	M. DZAMA / N. HESS / W. KENTRIDGE / N. RAUCH / D. RICHTER
			POETIC	12	C. AOSHIMA / J. DAMASCENO / V. DAWSON / P. DOIG / T. EITEL / I. ESSENHIGH / K. KILIMNIK / J.-M. OTHONIEL / M. PLESSEN / N. RIKA / D. ROTH / H. SUGITO / TAL R / F. TOMASELLI / YANG FUDONG	C. AOSHIMA / J. DAMASCENO / E. DAVID / V. DAWSON / P. DOIG / I. ESSENHIGH / J. JUST / K. KILIMNIK / G. MACUGA / K. MAMMA ANDERSSON / D. NOONAN / J. NORDSTRÖM / M. PLESSEN / C. ROJAS / A. STRBA / H. SUGITO / TAL R / G. & U. TOBIAS / A. WEKUA / YANG FUDONG
	PLAY	LIGHT-HEARTED	MARKETING	13	W. DELVOYE / DUBOSSARSKY & VINOGRADOV / U. FISCHER / J. KOONS / M. LECKEY / T. MURAKAMI / J. RHOADES / T. SACHS	A. DA CUNHA / W. DELVOYE / U. FISCHER / M. LECKEY / T. MURAKAMI / J. RHOADES / T. SACHS
			DIY	14	GELITIN / M. HANDFORTH / U. KRISANAMIS / G. KURI / J. LAMBIE / LOS CARPINTEROS / C. MARCLAY / V. MUNIZ / A. OEHLEN	C. ARCANGEL / CAO FEI / P. COFFIN / R. CUOGHI / L. ESTÉVE / GELITIN / M. HANDFORTH / J. HODGES / J. LAMBIE / C. MARCLAY / D. MULLER / V. MUNIZ / P. PIVI / R. RHODE / S. SHEARER / P. WHITE
		MORBID	ENVIRONMENTS	15	M. CATTELAN / ELMGREEN & DRAGSET / D. HIRST / R. KUSMIROWSKI / P. PARRENO / U. RONDINONE / M. WEINSTEIN	M. BOYCE / M. CATTELAN / P. CHAN / M. DAY-JACKSON / ELMGREEN & DRAGSET / D. HIRST / P. PARRENO / M-T. PERRET / U. RONDINONE / M. SCHINWALD / B. VIOLETTE / T. ZIPP
			HYBRIDIZATION	16	C. AMORALES / M. BARNEY / K. EDMIER / E. GALLAGHER / C. HOLSTAD / C. JAMIE / NOBLE & WEBSTER / T. SCHÜTTE / A. VAREJÃO	D. ALTMEJD / C. AMORALES / M. BARNEY / J. & D. CHAPMAN / E. GALLAGHER / C. HOLSTAD / M. MONAHAN / W. MUTU / NOBLE & WEBSTER / S. RUBY / A. VAREJÃO
EXPERIENCING	SELF	PERSONAL MYTH	METAPHYSICAL PROJECT	17	R. ACKERMANN / J. ANTONI / CAI GUO-QIANG / T. HIRSCHHORN / T. KOH / M. MANDERS / M. MORI	CAI GUO-QIANG / T. HIRSCHHORN / T. KOH / M. MANDERS / J. MEESE / M. MORI / P. NOBLE / C. SANDISON
			SOCIALLY ENGAGED	18	K. GEERS / M. LAURETTE / S. NESHAT	G. EIDE EINARSSON / K. GEERS / LINDER / S. NESHAT
		PERSONAL DRAMA	ROLE-PLAY	19	F. ALŸS / E. ANTILLE / C. BREITZ / O. BREUNING / D. GORDON / R. GRAHAM / I. & E. KABAKOV / S. LANDERS / M. MARSHALL / Y. MORIMURA / Y. NARA / J. OPIE / J. SHAW / L. SIMPSON / G. WEARING	F. ALŸS / C. BREITZ / O. BREUNING / P. CHANG / D. GORDON / I. & E. KABAKOV / Y. MORIMURA / Y. NARA / J. OPIE / G. WEARING / YAN LEI
			FACTUAL NARRATIVE	20	E-L. AHTILA / M. CREED / T. EMIN / P. GRAHAM / S. MCQUEEN / J. MONK / A. PACI / R. STINGEL	E-L. AHTILA / M. CREED / T. EMIN / L. FOWLER / P. GRAHAM / J. MAGID / S. MCQUEEN / A. PACI / G. SHAW / R. STINGEL
	BODY		STAGING	21	A. ABDESSEMED / D. BAECHLER / R. BALLEN / V. BEECROFT / C. BOURSIER-MOUGENOT / M. CANTOR / G. CREWDSON / P-L. DICORCIA / R. GANDER / R. ISLAM / B. MIKHAILOV / MUNTEAN & ROSENBLUM / J. ONOFRE / M. QUINN / A. SALA / D. SHRIGLEY / Y. SONE / S. TAYLOR-WOOD / J. TELLER / E. TEMPLETON / J. WALL / E. WURM	A. ABDESSEMED / T.L. AUAD / R. BALLEN / J. BILLING / T. BURR / M. CANTOR / G. CREWDSON / P-L. DICORCIA / R. GANDER / R. ISLAM / K. LIDÉN / K. MARTIN / MUNTEAN & ROSENBLUM / J. PIERSON / M. QUINN / A. SALA / T. SARACENO / T. SEHGAL / D. SHRIGLEY / Y. SONE / M. SOSNOWSKA / S. SZE / S. TAYLOR-WOOD / A. THAUBERGER / E. WURM
		FRAGILITY	AURATIC PRESENCE	22	D. AITKEN / H. AKAKÇE / K. ASDAM / M. BALKA / S. BALKENHOL / M. BORREMANS / P. BRADSHAW / J.-M. BUSTAMANTE / R. DIJKSTRA / M. DUMAS / A. FUSS / A. GALLACCIO / M. GALLACE / R. GOBER / M. HATOUM / J-A. KOO / V. KOSHLIAKOV / LEE BUL / P. MORRISON / R. MUECK / G. OROZCO / E. PEYTON / C. PIENE / J. PLENSA / M. RAEDECKER / B. ŠARČEVIĆ / F. TAN / W. TILLMANS / L. TUYMANS / S. TYKKÄ / R. WHITEREAD / C. WOOL / R. WRIGHT	D. AITKEN / H. AKAKÇE / M. BALKA / S. BALKENHOL / M. BORREMANS / L. CECCHINI / M. DUMAS / M. GALLACE / R. GOBER / A. GRANAT / M. HATOUM / G. HILDEBRANDT / S. JENSEN / A. KANWAR / J-A. KOO / LEE BUL / H. MIRRA / R. MUECK / R. NASHASHIBI / G. OROZCO / E. PEYTON / S. PHILIPSZ / C. RAY / E. ROTHSCHILD / D. STEWEN / B. STREULI / F. TAN / W. TILLMANS / L. TUYMANS / S. TYKKÄ / R. WHITEREAD / C. WOOL / R. WRIGHT / YAN PEI-MING / ZHANG XIAOGANG
		PLEASURE	SENSUALITY	23	C. BROWN / J. CURRIN / K. GROSSE / A. HERRERA / G. HUME / M. LIN / E. NETO / L. OWENS / P. RIST / T. SCHEIBITZ / J. TSCHÄPE / S. WILLIAMS	C. BROWN / K. GROSSE / A. HERRERA / G. HUME / D. MARTIN / E. NETO / L. OWENS / P. RIST / T. SCHEIBITZ / J. TSCHÄPE
			TRASHINESS	24	M. BONVICINI / S. LUCAS / F. MARCACCIO / P. MCCARTHY / J. SAVILLE / G. SCHNEIDER	M. BONVICINI / B. DE BRUYCKERE / S. LUCAS / C. OFILI / G. SCHNEIDER

means   international artists

SET/OBJECT/IMAGE				#	2003-2005	2006-2008
SET	CONTEXTUAL	WORK-ENVIRONMENT RELATIONSHIP	CLINICAL	1	DE ROOIJ (DE RIJKE & DE ROOIJ <2006) / O. ELIASSON / L. GILLICK / S. MORRIS / J. PARDO / P. PFEIFFER / T. REHBERGER	M. BARTOLINI / DE ROOIJ / I.DO ESPERITO SANTO / O. ELIASSON / L. GILLICK / S. MORRIS / J. PARDO / P. PFEIFFER / T. REHBERGER
			DREAMLIKE	2	F. ACKERMANN / H. AKAKÇE / D. ALMOND / C. AOSHIMA / M. BARNEY / M. BUCKINGHAM / J. CARDIFF / J. DODGE / M. DZAMA / S. FINCH / R. GANDER / P. HUYGHE / A. V. JANSSENS / I. & E. KABAKOV / W. KENTRIDGE / K. KILIMNIK / W. J. LIM / M. LIN / L. MCKENZIE / P. PARRENO / J. PLENSA / A. SALA / J. SHAW / SUI-MEI TSE / D. THATER / Ka. WALKER / R. WRIGHT / C. WYN EVANS	H. AKAKÇE / D. ALMOND / C. AOSHIMA / M. BARNEY / M. BUCKINGHAM / J. CARDIFF / P. COFFIN / E. DAVID / J. DODGE / M. DZAMA / L. ERLICH / L. ESTÈVE / S. FINCH / R. GANDER / J. HODGES / P. HUYGHE / I. & E. KABAKOV / W. KENTRIDGE / K. KILIMNIK / W. J. LIM / D. MALJKOVIĆ / L. MCKENZIE / P. PARRENO / S. PHILIPSZ / A. SALA / C. SANDISON / D. THATER / C. VON BONIN / Ka. WALKER / A. WEKUA / R. WRIGHT / C. YASS
		WORK-VISITOR RELATIONSHIP	PLAYFUL	3	O. BREUNING / M. CATTELAN / M. CREED / ELMGREEN & DRAGSET / U. FISCHER / C. FLOYER / GELITIN / R. GRAHAM / J. HEIN / C. HÖLLER / C. JANKOWSKI / S. LANDERS / J. MONK / Y. MORIMURA / R. NEUESCHWANDER / D. SHRIGLEY / A. SLOMINSKI / P. UKLANSKI / E. WURM	C. ARCANGEL / O. BREUNING / M. CATTELAN / M. CREED / M. CUEVAS / R. CUOGHI / ELMGREEN & DRAGSET / U. FISCHER / C. FLOYER / C. FONTAINE / GELITIN / J. HEIN / C. HÖLLER / C. JANKOWSKI / J. MACCHI / MAREPE / Y. MORIMURA / R. NEUESCHWANDER / D. PERJOVSCHI / P. PIVI / P. REYES / D. SHRIGLEY / SUPERFLEX / E. WURM
			HOSTILE	4	M. BONVICINI / A. BULLOCH / T. HIRSCHHORN / S. LUCAS / J. RHOADES / G. SCHNEIDER / S. SIERRA / J. WOHNSEIFER / A. ZITTEL	M. BONVICINI / J. & D. CHAPMAN / G. EIDE EINARSSON / T. HIRSCHHORN / S. LUCAS / J. RHOADES / G. SCHNEIDER / A. ZITTEL
	ASSOCIATING AN ACTION	TRACES	REMAINS	5	K. GROSSE / B. MCGEE	ATLAS GROUP (WALID RAAD) / J. BILLING / P. BISMUTH / J. DE COCK / J. DELLER / L. FOWLER / K. GROSSE / J. KOESTER / B. MCGEE / J. SMITH / R. SPAULINGS
			ICONIC	6	E. ANTILLE / A. BOWERS / A. BUBLEX / V. MUNIZ / J. NGUYEN-HATSUSHJBA / M. OHANIAN / S. STARLING / M. STEVENSON	A. BOWERS / A. GRANAT / J. MAGID / H. MIRRA / V. MUNIZ / J. NGUYEN-HATSUSHJBA / M. OHANIAN / S. STARLING / M. STEVENSON
		LIVE	ALLEGORY	7	F. ALŸS / J. ANTONI / K. ASDAM / V. BEECROFT / P. MCCARTHY / S. MCQUEEN / J. ONOFRE / S. PREGO / R. TIRAVANIJA	ALLORA & CALZADILLA / F. ALŸS / ASSUME VIVID ASTRO POCUS / T. BRUGUERA / J.HANNING / S. MCQUEEN / R. ONDÁK / T. SEHGAL / R. TIRAVANIJA
			THE INDIVIDUAL	8	J. BOCK / A. FRASER / KIMSOOJA / T. KOH / M. LAURETTE	J. BOCK / P. CHANG / A. FRASER / KIMSOOJA / T. KOH / D. MARTIN / J. MEESE / R. RHODE
OBJECT	SACRALIZED	TECHNICAL CHARACTER	COLLECTIVE UNCONSCIOUS	9	J. KOONS / T. MURAKAMI / J. OPIE	T. MURAKAMI / J. OPIE / D. PFLUMM
			INDIVIDUAL UNCONSCIOUS	10	CAI GUO-QIANG / W. DELVOYE / T. FERNÁNDEZ / D. GORDON / D. HIRST / M. MORI / R. MUECK / J.-M. OTHONIEL / M. QUINN	CAI GUO-QIANG / W. DELVOYE / D. GORDON / D. HIRST / M. MORI / R. MUECK / M. QUINN / C. RAY / E. ROTHSCHILD
		MANUAL PROCESS	METAPHYSICAL DIMENSION	11		D. ALTMEJD / L. CECCHINI / R. SHAW
			PAGAN DIMENSION	12	K. ALTHOFF / S. BALKENHOL / M. CANTOR / T. EMIN / A. GALLACCIO / C. JAMIE / U. KRISANAMIS / C. PARKER / D. ROTH / T. SCHÜTTE / Y. SONE	K. ALTHOFF / S. BALKENHOL / M. CANTOR / T. EMIN / Su. GUPTA / C. OFILI / S. RUBY / Y. SONE / G. & U. TOBIAS / P. WHITE
	HUMAN SCALE	VESTIGE	UTOPIAS	13	C. AMORALES / M. BAJEVIC / M. BALKA / J.-M. BUSTAMANTE / T. DONNELLY / G. GABELLONE / C. GARAICOA / W. GUYTON / HUANG YONG PING / V. KOSHLIAKOV / LEE BUL / M. MANDERS / J. MCELHENY / G. OROZCO / A. PACI / M. RAEDECKER / B. ŠARČEVIĆ / T. SCHEIBITZ / R. STINGEL / R. WHITEREAD	C. AMORALES / M. BALKA / T. DONNELLY / C. GARAICOA / W. GUYTON / HUANG YONG PING / S. JENSEN / LEE BUL / G. MACUGA / M. MANDERS / J. MCELHENY / M. MONAHAN / D. NOONAN / G. OROZCO / A. PACI / M-T. PERRET / T. PUTRIH / T. SCHEIBITZ / G. SIBONY / D. STEWEN / R. STINGEL / K. STRUNZ / N. WERMERS / R. WHITEREAD
			POP CULTURE	14	D. BAECHLER / P. BRADSHAW / S. CHETWYND / B. DAHLEM / M. DION / T. FRIEDMAN / M. HANDFORTH / R. HARRISON / J-A. HERNÁNDEZ-DÍEZ / N. HESS / J-A. KOO / G. KURI / R. KUSMIROWSKI / J. LAMBIE / M. LECKEY / G. LIGON / LOS CARPINTEROS / C. MARCLAY / NOBLE & WEBSTER / H. OP DE BEECK / T. SACHS / J. STOCKHOLDER / TAL R / E. TEMPLETON / K. TYSON / M. WEINSTEIN / WILCOX T. J. / C. WOOL	M. BOYCE / T. BURR / S. CHETWYND / A. DA CUNHA / M. DION / M. HANDFORTH / R. HARRISON / R. HAWKINS / L. HEMPEL / J-A. HERNÁNDEZ-DÍEZ / N. HESS / G. HILDEBRANDT / A. KELM / J-A. KOO / J. LAMBIE / M. LECKEY / K. LIDÉN / G. LIGON / C. MARCLAY / K. MARTIN / D. MULLER / NOBLE & WEBSTER / H. OP DE BEECK / G. PERRY / J. PIERSON / C. ROJAS / T. SACHS / S. SHEARER / J. STOCKHOLDER / S. SZE / TAL R / K. TYSON / B. VIOLETTE / Ke. WALKER / WANG DU / WILCOX T.J. / J. WOLFSON / C. WOOL
		THREAT/ PROTECTION RELATION	DRAMATIC	15	A. ABDESSEMED / S. DURANT / M. FRANÇOIS / K. GEERS / F. GYGI / M. HATOUM / R. ISLAM / I. MANGLANO-OVALLE / M. MARSHALL / P. MORRISON / S. NESHAT / D. ORTEGA / C. PIENE / U. RONDINONE / L. SCHNITGER / Y. SHONIBARE / S. XHAFA	A. ABDESSEMED / C. BÜCHEL / P. CHAN / N. COOKE / M. DAY-JACKSON / B. DE BRUYCKERE / N. DJURBERG / R. FEINSTEIN / K. GEERS / M. HATOUM / R. ISLAM / S. NESHAT / D. ORTEGA / U. RONDINONE / T. SARACENO / M. SCHINWALD / Y. SHONIBARE / M. SOSNOWSKA / S. XHAFA / T. ZIPP
			KINESTHETIC	16	G. AMER / C. BOURSIER-MOUGENOT / P. CABRITA REIS / J. DAMASCENO / K. EDMIER / A. ERKMEN / R. GOBER / C. HOLSTAD / C. IGLESIAS / F. MARCACCIO / B. MELGAARD / E. NETO / A. VAREJÃO	G. AMER / T. L. AUAD / J. DAMASCENO / R. GOBER / C. HOLSTAD / C. IGLESIAS / E. NETO / A. VAREJÃO
IMAGE	MOVING	MISE-EN-SCENE	DOCUMENTARY-STYLE	17	E-L. AHTILA / K. ATAMAN / Y. BARTANA / S. DOUGLAS / H. FAROCKI / E. JACIR / I. JULIEN / S. LOCKHART / A. MIK / L. SIMPSON / C. SULLIVAN / G. WEARING / J. & L. WILSON / A. ZMIJEWSKI	E-L. AHTILA / K. ATAMAN / Y. BARTANA / G. BYRNE / S. DOUGLAS / H. FAROCKI / O. FAST / E. JACIR / I. JULIEN / A. KANWAR / S. LOCKHART / A. MIK / C. SULLIVAN / A. THAUBERGER / G. WEARING / J. & L. WILSON / A. ZMIJEWSKI
			PARODIC	18	C. BREITZ / F. VEZZOLI	G. BEN-NER / C. BREITZ / CAO FEI / F. VEZZOLI
		STATE	SLOW TEMPO	19	D. AITKEN / T. DEAN / W. DOHERTY / HUBBARD & BIRCHLER / A. LARSSON / M. LEWIS / F. TAN / S. TAYLOR-WOOD / S. TYKKÄ / YANG FUDONG	D. AITKEN / D. CLAERBOUT / T. DEAN / HUBBARD & BIRCHLER / J. JUST / R. NASHASHIBI / A. STRBA / F. TAN / S. TAYLOR-WOOD / S. TYKKÄ / YANG FUDONG
			RAPID TEMPO	20	P. RIST	P. RIST
	STILL	AUTOMATED INTERMEDIARY	COLD USE	21	G. CREWDSON / T. DEMAND / P.-L. DICORCIA / R. DIJKSTRA / A. FUSS / P. GRAHAM / A. GURSKY / T. RUFF / T. SIMON / J. WALL	G. CREWDSON / T. DEMAND / P.-L. DICORCIA / P. GRAHAM / A. GURSKY / T. SIMON / B. STREULI
			VISCERAL USE	22	R. BALLEN / B. MIKHAILOV / N. RIKA / J. TELLER / W. TILLMANS	R. BALLEN / W. TILLMANS
			DRAWING	23	E. GALLAGHER / A. HERRERA / MUNTEAN & ROSENBLUM / Y.NARA / R. PETTIBON / F. TOMASELLI	E. GALLAGHER / A. HERRERA / LINDER / J. MEHRETU / MUNTEAN & ROSENBLUM / W. MUTU / Y. NARA / P. NOBLE / J. NORDSTRÖM / R. PETTIBON
		HAND-CRAFTED	PAINTING	24	R. ACKERMANN / M. BORREMANS / C. BROWN / J. CURRIN / V. DAWSON / P. DOIG / DUBOSSARSKY & VINOGRADOV / M. DUMAS / T. EITEL / I. ESSENHIGH / B. FRIZE / B. FURNAS / M. GALLACE / E. HAVEKOST / G. HUME / J. LASKER / A. OEHLEN / L. OWENS / E. PEYTON / R. PHILLIPS / M. PLESSEN / N. RAUCH / D. RICHTER / W. SASNAL / J. SAVILLE / H. SUGITO / J. TSCHÄPE / L. TUYMANS / S. WILLIAMS	T. ABTS / M. BORREMANS / C. BROWN / V. DAWSON / P. DOIG / M. DUMAS / I. ESSENHIGH / M. GALLACE / E. HAVEKOST / G. HUME / K. MAMMA ANDERSSON / J. MARTIN / L. OWENS / E. PEYTON / M. PLESSEN / N. RAUCH / D. RICHTER / W. SASNAL / G. SHAW / H. SUGITO / J. TSCHÄPE / L. TUYMANS / YAN LEI / YAN PEI-MING / ZHANG XIAOGANG / P. ZIMMERMAN

motors international artists

2009-2011

				#	Artists
UNDERSTANDING	PERCEPTION	LIMITS	TIME	1	M. BUCKINGHAM / D. CLAERBOUT / T. DEAN / T. DONNELLY / P. ESQUIVIAS / S. LOCKHART / J. MACCHI / D. MALJKOVIĆ / J. MANČUŠKA / S. STARLING / T. VONNA MICHELL
			SPACE	2	M. BARTOLINI / L. ERLICH / A. GURSKY / J. HEIN / HUBBARD & BIRCHLER / J. MEHRETU / R. ONDÁK / D. ORTEGA / J. PARDO / T. PUTRIH / O. TUAZON
		MECHANISMS	FORMAT TRANSPOSITION	3	D. CAMPBELL / DE ROOIJ (DE RIJKE & DE ROOIJ <2006) / T. DEMAND / O. FAST / C. FLOYER / W. GONZALES / W. GUYTON / J. MCELHENY / P. PFEIFFER / W. SASNAL
			SENSORY EXPERIENCE	4	T. ABTS / J. CARDIFF / J. DODGE / O. ELIASSON / C. HÖLLER
	SOCIETY/CODES	CONDITIONING	MIMESIS	5	K. ATAMAN / Y. BARTANA / F. BRYCE / G. BYRNE / V. CARRON / J. DELLER / L. GILLICK / Su. GUPTA / J. MECKSEPER / A. MIK / S. MORRIS / M. NELSON / M. PERNICE / S. SIERRA / J. SMITH / S. SNYDER / C. SULLIVAN / SUPERFLEX / F. VEZZOLI / Ke. WALKER / XU ZHEN (MADEIN) / A. ZITTEL / A. ZMIJEWSKI
			DERISION	6	ALLORA & CALZADILLA / M. DION / C. FONTAINE / C. GARAICOA / R. HARRISON / J. HOROWITZ / C. JANKOWSKI / L. MCKENZIE / R. PETTIBON / G. TURK / S. XHAFA
		UNJUST/ EXCLUSIONARY	ACTS OF SHARING	7	E. ARAKAWA / ASSUME VIVID ASTRO POCUS / HUANG YONG PING / KIMSOOJA / MAREPE / R. NEUESCHWANDER / P. REYES / R. TIRAVANIJA / C. VON BONIN / A. WEERASETHAKUL
			DENUNCIATION	8	E. ARCENEAUX / ATLAS GROUP (WALID RAAD) / A. BOWERS / H. FAROCKI / I. JULIEN / D. PERJOVSCHI / Y. SHONIBARE / T. SIMON / D. THATER / Ka. WALKER / J. & L. WILSON
DOING	NARRATION	GROTESQUE	PARODIC	9	J. BOCK / S. CHETWYND / T. FRIEDMAN / B. MCGEE
			DISQUIETING	10	ANDY HOPE 1930/ J. DE BALINCOURT / N. DJURBERG / B. MELGAARD / R. SHAW / M. WEBER
		DREAMLIKE	DRAMATIC	11	M. DZAMA / W. KENTRIDGE / N. RAUCH
			POETIC	12	E. DAVID / V. DAWSON / P. DOIG / J. JUST / K. KILIMNIK / K. KRISTALOVA / G. MACUGA / D. NOONAN / J. NORDSTRÖM / P. OLOWSKA / J.-M. OTHONIEL / A. STRBA / H. SUGITO / U. VON BRANDENBURG / A. WEKUA / YANG FUDONG
	PLAY	LIGHT-HEARTED	MARKETING	13	S. DENNY / D. LIESKE / T. MURAKAMI / A. REYLE
			DIY	14	C. ARCANGEL / CAO FEI / P. COFFIN / D. COLEN / R. CUOGHI / GELITIN / F. HERRERO / J. HODGES / G. KURI / J. LAMBIE / R. PRUITT / R. RHODE / M. SAILSTORFER / S. SHEARER
		MORBID	ENVIRONMENTS	15	M. CATTELAN / P. CHAN / M. DAY-JACKSON / D. GONZALEZ-FOERSTER / R. HIORNS / D. HIRST / P. PARRENO / M-T. PERRET / U. RONDINONE / T. TROUVÉ / B. VIOLETTE
			HYBRIDIZATION	16	D. ALTMEJD / C. AMORALES / M. BARNEY / G. BROWN / A. CURRY / G. FARMER / E. GALLAGHER / N. HLOBO / R. JOHNSON / J. KALLAT / W. MUTU / R. TRECARTIN / C. WILKES
EXPERIENCING	SELF	PERSONAL MYTH	METAPHYSICAL PROJECT	17	J. ANTONI / CAI GUO-QIANG / DO-HO SUH / T. HIRSCHHORN / T. KOH / M. MANDERS / J. MEESE / QIU ZHIJIE / C. SANDISON
			SOCIALLY ENGAGED	18	AI WEIWEI / G. EIDE EINARSSON / S. LANDAU / T. MARGOLLES / S. NESHAT / D. VO / K. WILEY
		PERSONAL DRAMA	ROLE-PLAY	19	F. ALŸS / C. BREITZ / P. BRONSTEIN / K. CYTTER / D. GORDON / R. KJARTANSSON / T. LEE / K. LINZY / A. RUILOVA / J. SHAW / G. VAN DER WERVE / E. WARDILL
			FACTUAL NARRATIVE	20	E-L. AHTILA / J. ARANDA / BERNARDETTE CORPORATION / M. BOUROUISSA / A. CESARCO / A. COLLIER / J. COLOMER / M. CREED / M. DAVEY / T. EMIN / L. FOWLER / M. GARCIA-TORRES / P. GRAHAM / J. MAGID / J. MONK / A. ÖĞÜT / A. PACI / QUAYTMAN R .H. / K. ŠEDÁ
	BODY	FRAGILITY	STAGING	21	A. ABDESSEMED / R. BALLEN / A. BIRCKEN / J. BORNSTEIN / C. BOURSIER-MOUGENOT / T. BURR / M. CANTOR / G. CREWDSON / A. CRUZVILLEGAS / R. GANDER / R. ISLAM / K. LIDÉN / K. MARTIN / B. MIKHAILOV / J-L. MYLAYNE / J. PIERSON / M. QUINN / A. SALA / T. SARACENO / T. SEHGAL / D. SHRIGLEY / M. SOSNOWSKA / S. SZE / E. WURM / H. YANG
			AURATIC PRESENCE	22	D. AITKEN / M. BALKA / W. BESHTY / M. BORREMANS / S. BRADLEY / M. BRANNON / M. DEAN / S. DONG / H. EPAMINONDA / W. FORD / C. GAILLARD / M. GALLACE / Sh. GUPTA / S. HEFUNA / D. HERNÁNDEZ / S. JENSEN / A. KANWAR / I. KIAER / J-A. KOO / LEE BUL / N. LOWMAN / H. MIRRA / M. MOTI / G. OROZCO / E. PEYTON / S. PHILIPSZ / S. PRICE / E. ROTHSCHILD / J. TICHY / W. TILLMANS / L. TUYMANS / R. WHITEREAD / C. WOOL / YAN PEI-MING / ZHANG ENLI / ZHANG XIAOGANG
		PLEASURE	SENSUALITY	23	D. BELL / C. BROWN / FENG ZHENGJIE / K. GROSSE / G. HUME / E. LASSRY / M. NEPOMUCENO / E. NETO / L. OWENS / P. RIST / T. SCHEIBITZ / J. TSCHÄPE / L. YUSKAVAGE
			TRASHINESS	24	M. BONVICINI / B. DE BRUYCKERE / V. MAN / G. SCHNEIDER / D. SCHUTZ

means international artists

2009-2011

SET/OBJECT/IMAGE			Category	#	Artists
SET	CONTEXTUAL	WORK-ENVIRONMENT RELATIONSHIP	CLINICAL	1	M. BARTOLINI / DE ROOIJ (DE RIJKE & DE ROOIJ <2006) / O. ELIASSON / L. GILLICK / S. MORRIS / J. PARDO / P. PFEIFFER
			DREAMLIKE	2	ANDY HOPE 1930/ M. BARNEY / M. BUCKINGHAM / J. CARDIFF / P. COFFIN / E. DAVID / J. DODGE / M. DZAMA / L. ERLICH / R. GANDER / D. GONZALEZ-FOERSTER / J. HODGES / W. KENTRIDGE / K. KILIMNIK / D. MALJKOVIĆ / L. MCKENZIE / P. PARRENO / S. PHILIPSZ / A. SALA / C. SANDISON / J. SHAW / D. THATER / J. TICHY / C. VON BONIN / Ka. WALKER / A. WEKUA
		WORK-VISITOR RELATIONSHIP	PLAYFUL	3	C. ARCANGEL / M. CATTELAN / A. CESARCO / M. CREED / R. CUOGHI / C. FLOYER / C. FONTAINE / GELITIN / J. HEIN / C. HÖLLER / C. JANKOWSKI / T. LEE / J. MACCHI / MAREPE / J. MONK / R. NEUESCHWANDER / A. ÖĞÜT / D. PERJOVSCHI / P. REYES / D. SHRIGLEY / SUPERFLEX / G. TURK / M. WEBER / E. WURM / XU ZHEN (MADEIN)
			HOSTILE	4	M. BONVICINI / G. EIDE EINARSSON / T. HIRSCHHORN / J. MECKSEPER / G. SCHNEIDER / S. SIERRA / A. ZITTEL
	ASSOCIATING AN ACTION	TRACES	REMAINS	5	ATLAS GROUP (WALID RAAD) / J. DELLER / P. ESQUIVIAS / L. FOWLER / K. GROSSE / F. HERRERO / B. MCGEE / K. ŠEDÁ / J. SMITH
			ICONIC	6	AI WEIWEI / A. BOWERS / A. COLLIER / M. DAVEY / M. GARCIA-TORRES / J. MAGID / H. MIRRA / S. SNYDER / S. STARLING / G. VAN DER WERVE
		LIVE	ALLEGORY	7	ALLORA & CALZADILLA / F. ALŸS / J. ANTONI / E. ARAKAWA / ASSUME VIVID ASTRO POCUS / J. COLOMER / K. CYTTER / R. ONDÁK / T. SEHGAL / R. TIRAVANIJA / A. WEERASETHAKUL
			THE INDIVIDUAL	8	J. BOCK / KIMSOOJA / R. KJARTANSSON / T. KOH / K. LINZY / J. MEESE / QIUZHIJIE / R. RHODE / T. VONNA MICHELL
OBJECT	SACRALIZED	TECHNICAL CHARACTER	COLLECTIVE UNCONSCIOUS	9	T. MURAKAMI
			INDIVIDUAL UNCONSCIOUS	10	CAI GUO-QIANG / DO-HO SUH / D. GORDON / D. HIRST / J.-M. OTHONIEL / M. QUINN / E. ROTHSCHILD
		MANUAL PROCESS	METAPHYSICAL DIMENSION	11	D. ALTMEJD / R. SHAW
			PAGAN DIMENSION	12	M. CANTOR / T. EMIN / Su. GUPTA / V. MAN
	HUMAN SCALE	VESTIGE	UTOPIAS	13	C. AMORALES / J. ARANDA / M. BALKA / BERNARDETTE CORPORATION / A. BIRCKEN / J. BORNSTEIN / P. BRONSTEIN / D. CAMPBELL / V. CARRON / A. CURRY / M. DEAN / T. DONNELLY / H. EPAMINONDA / C. GAILLARD / C. GARAICOA / W. GUYTON / S. HEFUNA / HUANG YONG PING / S. JENSEN / R. JOHNSON / I. KIAER / LEE BUL / D. LIESKE / G. MACUGA / J. MANČUŠKA / M. MANDERS / J. MCELHENY / M. MOTI / M. NELSON / D. NOONAN / P. OLOWSKA / G. OROZCO / A. PACI / M. PERNICE / M-T. PERRET / T. PUTRIH / QUAYTMAN R .H. / T. SCHEIBITZ / T. TROUVÉ / O. TUAZON / D. VO / U. VON BRANDENBURG / R. WHITEREAD / H. YANG
			POP CULTURE	14	E. ARCENEAUX / W. BESHTY / S. BRADLEY / T. BURR / S. CHETWYND / D. COLEN / S. DENNY / M. DION / S. DONG / T. FRIEDMAN / R. HARRISON / D. HERNÁNDEZ / J. HOROWITZ / J-A. KOO / G. KURI / J. LAMBIE / E. LASSRY / K. LIDÉN / N. LOWMAN / K. MARTIN / J. PIERSON / S. PRICE / R. PRUITT / A. REYLE / S. SHEARER / S. SZE / R. TRECARTIN / B. VIOLETTE / Ke. WALKER / C. WILKES / C. WOOL / ZHANG ENLI
		THREAT/ PROTECTION RELATION	DRAMATIC	15	A. ABDESSEMED / P. CHAN / A. CRUZVILLEGAS / M. DAY-JACKSON / B. DE BRUYCKERE / N. DJURBERG / G. FARMER / Sh. GUPTA / R. ISLAM / J. KALLAT / K. KRISTALOVA / T. MARGOLLES / S. NESHAT / D. ORTEGA / U. RONDINONE / M. SAILSTORFER / T. SARACENO / Y. SHONIBARE / M. SOSNOWSKA / E. WARDILL / S. XHAFA
			KINESTHETIC	16	C. BOURSIER-MOUGENOT / M. BRANNON / R. HIORNS / N. HLOBO / S. LANDAU / B. MELGAARD / M. NEPOMUCENO / E. NETO
IMAGE	MOVING	MISE-EN-SCENE	DOCUMENTARY-STYLE	17	E-L. AHTILA / K. ATAMAN / Y. BARTANA / M. BOUROUISSA / G. BYRNE / H. FAROCKI / O. FAST / I. JULIEN / A. KANWAR / S. LOCKHART / A. MIK / C. SULLIVAN / J. & L. WILSON / A. ZMIJEWSKI
			PARODIC	18	C. BREITZ / CAO FEI / F. VEZZOLI
		STATE	SLOW TEMPO	19	D. AITKEN / D. CLAERBOUT / T. DEAN / HUBBARD & BIRCHLER / J. JUST / A. STRBA / YANG FUDONG
			RAPID TEMPO	20	P. RIST / A. RUILOVA
	STILL	AUTOMATED INTERMEDIARY	COLD USE	21	G. CREWDSON / T. DEMAND / P. GRAHAM / A. GURSKY / J-L. MYLAYNE / T. SIMON
			VISCERAL USE	22	R. BALLEN / B. MIKHAILOV / W. TILLMANS
		HAND-CRAFTED	DRAWING	23	F. BRYCE / W. FORD / E. GALLAGHER / J. MEHRETU / W. MUTU / J. NORDSTRÖM / R. PETTIBON
			PAINTING	24	T. ABTS / D. BELL / M. BORREMANS / C. BROWN / G. BROWN / V. DAWSON / J. DE BALINCOURT / P. DOIG / FENG ZHENGJIE / M. GALLACE / W. GONZALES / G. HUME / L. OWENS / E. PEYTON / N. RAUCH / W. SASNAL / D. SCHUTZ / H. SUGITO / J. TSCHÄPE / L. TUYMANS / K. WILEY/ YAN PEI-MING / L. YUSKAVAGE / ZHANG XIAOGANG

motors French artists

1987-2011

UNDERSTANDING	PERCEPTION	LIMITS	TIME	1	R. AUGUSTE-DORMEUIL / É. CHAMBAUD / M. DELBECQ / M. FORTUNÉ P. HUYGHE / B. MAIRE / N. MOULIN / M. OHANIAN PUGNAIRE & RAFFINI
			SPACE	2	E. BALLET / D. BLAIS / S. COUTURIER / M. GEFFRIAUD V. LAMOUROUX / P. MALPHETTES
		MECHANISMS	FORMAT TRANSPOSITION	3	W. ALMENDRA / P.-O. ARNAUD / C. BENZAKEN / P. COGNÉE D. COINDET / DETANICO & LAIN / N. FLOC'H / V. JOUMARD B. PERRAMANT / D. PETITGAND / B. PIFFARETTI / P. PINAUD E. RICHER / TURSIC & MILLE / X. VEILHAN / R. ZARKA
			SENSORY EXPERIENCE	4	D. BALULA / C. BART / D. FIGARELLA / B. FRIZE
	SOCIETY/CODES	CONDITIONING	MIMESIS	5	O. BARDIN / A. DECLERCQ / V. JOUVE / V. MRÉJÉN B. SERRALONGUE / SOCIÉTÉ RÉALISTE / WANG DU
			DERISION	6	P. ARDOUVIN / F. BAGHRICHE / S. BÉRARD / P. BISMUTH A. BUBLEX / C. CLOSKY / O. DOLLINGER / S. ENGRAMER C. FONTAINE / A. FROMENT / J. HUBAUT / P. JOSEPH A. LABELLE-ROJOUX / M. LE CHEVALLIER / A. PERIGOT / J. PRÉVIEUX C. RUTAULT
		UNJUST/ EXCLUSIONARY	ACTS OF SHARING	7	S. BLOCHER / HUANG YONG PING / R. TIRAVANIJA
			DENUNCIATION	8	ART ORIENTÉ OBJET / P. CONVERT / M. FARRELL / D. FIUZA-FAUSTINO
DOING	NARRATION	GROTESQUE	PARODIC	9	D. FIRMAN / T. MOUILLÉ / V. YASSEF
			DISQUIETING	10	L. REYNAUD-DEWAR / A. SÉCHAS
		DREAMLIKE	DRAMATIC	11	
			POETIC	12	M. BRIAND / BRUANT & SPANGARO / L. MONTARON / O. NOTELLET TIXADOR & POINCHEVAL / U. VON BRANDENBURG
	PLAY	LIGHT-HEARTED	MARKETING	13	É. BOSSUT / F. CURLET / M. MERCIER / B. PEINADO F. SCURTI
			DIY	14	K. BISCH / S. CALAIS / DEWAR & GICQUEL / R. FAUGUET K. SOLOMOUKHA
		MORBID	ENVIRONMENTS	15	BERDAGUER & PÉJUS / D. GONZALEZ-FOERSTER / L. GRASSO / L. GRÉAUD B. LAMARCHE / C. LÉVÊQUE / D. MAZIÈRES / P. PARRENO T. TROUVÉ
			HYBRIDIZATION	16	É. BAUDART / M. BLAZY / D. DEROUBAIX / S. ROUSSEAU J-L. VERNA
EXPERIENCING	SELF	PERSONAL MYTH	METAPHYSICAL PROJECT	17	T. HIRSCHHORN / Y. SALOMONE / N. TALEC
			SOCIALLY ENGAGED	18	M. LAURETTE / P. THOMAS / A. THURNAUER
		PERSONAL DRAMA	ROLE-PLAY	19	G. BARBIER / V. BARRÉ / V. BELIN / O. BLANCKART B. DELLSPERGER / V. FAVRE / P. PERROT / A-M. SCHNEIDER
			FACTUAL NARRATIVE	20	É. LEVÉ / P. SORIN / G.T. STOLL / D. TATAH
	BODY		STAGING	21	R. BOURNIGAULT / C. BOURSIER-MOUGENOT / V. CORPET / C. HENROT A. LECCIA / P. LEGUILLON / J-L. MOULÈNE / J-L. MYLAYNE G. PANCHAL / G. PARIS / É. PITOISET / É. POITEVIN P. RAMETTE / A. SALA
		FRAGILITY	AURATIC PRESENCE	22	K. ATTIA / D. CABANES / M. DESGRANDCHAMPS / C. GAILLARD J-A. KOO / G. LEBLON / R. LERICOLAIS / N. LESUEUR D. MARCEL / S. THIDET / YAN PEI-MING
		PLEASURE	SENSUALITY	23	R. KOLLE / P. MAYAUX
			TRASHINESS	24	A. MOLINERO / S. PENCHRÉAC'H

means   French artists

1987-2011

SET/OBJECT/IMAGE	Category	Subcategory	Type	#	Artists
SET	CONTEXTUAL	WORK-ENVIRONMENT RELATIONSHIP	CLINICAL	1	C. BART / V. JOUMARD / D. PETITGAND / C. RUTAULT / SOCIÉTÉ RÉALISTE
			DREAMLIKE	2	E. BALLET / D. GONZALEZ-FOERSTER / L. GRASSO / L. GRÉAUD / P. HUYGHE / B. LAMARCHE / A. LECCIA / C. LÉVÊQUE / P. MALPHETTES / D. MAZIÉRES / P. PARRENO / A. SALA
		WORK-VISITOR RELATIONSHIP	PLAYFUL	3	P. ARDOUVIN / G. BARBIER / S. BÉRARD / BERDAGUER & PÉJUS / C. CLOSKY / DETANICO & LAIN / O. DOLLINGER / S. ENGRAMER / R. FAUGUET / C. FONTAINE / A. FROMENT / J. HUBAUT / P. JOSEPH / A. LABELLE-ROJOUX / V. LAMOUROUX / M. LE CHEVALLIER / É. LEVÉ / P. MAYAUX / O. NOTELLET / G. PARIS / A. PERIGOT / J. PRÉVIEUX / A. SÉCHAS / K. SOLOMOUKHA / P. THOMAS
			HOSTILE	4	M. FARRELL / T. HIRSCHHORN
	ASSOCIATING AN ACTION	TRACES	REMAINS	5	ART ORIENTÉ OBJET / F. BAGHRICHE / P. BISMUTH / R. BOURNIGAULT / A. DECLERCQ / R. LERICOLAIS / P. PINAUD / PUGNAIRE & RAFFINI / Y. SALOMONE
			ICONIC	6	D. BALULA / A. BUBLEX / M. DELBECQ / N. FLOC'H / L. MONTARON / M. OHANIAN / G.T. STOLL
		LIVE	ALLEGORY	7	O. BARDIN / M. BLAZY / M. BRIAND / BRUANT & SPANGARO / N. TALEC / R. TIRAVANIJA
			THE INDIVIDUAL	8	M. LAURETTE
OBJECT	SACRALIZED	TECHNICAL CHARACTER	COLLECTIVE UNCONSCIOUS	9	P. CONVERT / X. VEILHAN
			INDIVIDUAL UNCONSCIOUS	10	
		MANUAL PROCESS	METAPHYSICAL DIMENSION	11	G. PANCHAL
			PAGAN DIMENSION	12	L. REYNAUD-DEWAR
	HUMAN SCALE	VESTIGE	UTOPIAS	13	P.-O. ARNAUD / R. AUGUSTE-DORMEUIL / K. BISCH / S. CALAIS / É. CHAMBAUD / C. GAILLARD / M. GEFFRIAUD / C. HENROT / HUANG YONG PING / G. LEBLON / B. MAIRE / D. MARCEL / J-L. MOULÈNE / E. RICHER / TIXADOR & POINCHEVAL / T. TROUVÉ / U. VON BRANDENBURG / R. ZARKA
			POP CULTURE	14	W. ALMENDRA / V. BARRÉ / É. BAUDART / O. BLANCKART / É. BOSSUT / D. COINDET / F. CURLET / D. DEROUBAIX / DEWAR & GICQUEL / J-A. KOO / P. LEGUILLON / M. MERCIER / B. PEINADO / S. ROUSSEAU / F. SCURTI / A. THURNAUER / WANG DU / V. YASSEF
		THREAT/ PROTECTION RELATION	DRAMATIC	15	K. ATTIA / D. FIRMAN / D. FIUZA-FAUSTINO / T. MOUILLÉ / É. PITOISET / P. RAMETTE
			KINESTHETIC	16	D. BLAIS / C. BOURSIER-MOUGENOT / D. CABANES / D. FIGARELLA / A. MOLINERO / S. THIDET
IMAGE	MOVING	MISE-EN-SCENE	DOCUMENTARY-STYLE	17	S. BLOCHER / V. MRÉJÉN
			PARODIC	18	B. DELLSPERGER / P. SORIN
		STATE	SLOW TEMPO	19	M. FORTUNÉ
			RAPID TEMPO	20	
	STILL	AUTOMATED INTERMEDIARY	COLD USE	21	V. BELIN / S. COUTURIER / V. JOUVE / N. LESUEUR / N. MOULIN / J-L. MYLAYNE / É. POITEVIN / B. SERRALONGUE
			VISCERAL USE	22	
		HAND-CRAFTED	DRAWING	23	A-M. SCHNEIDER / J-L. VERNA
			PAINTING	24	C. BENZAKEN / P. COGNÉE / V. CORPET / M. DESGRANDCHAMPS / V. FAVRE / B. FRIZE / R. KOLLE / S. PENCHRÉAC'H / B. PERRAMANT / P. PERROT / B. PIFFARETTI / D. TATAH / TURSIC & MILLE / YAN PEI-MING

applying the results

The results presented in the charts and appendices can be used for the following purposes:

SITUATING AN ARTIST FEATURED IN THE STUDY

Go to the Index of Artists p. 67. The Index provides information on each artist's Motor-Means pair, on the art scenes they are involved in and the periods they feature in.

Then go to the corresponding Motors and Means Charts or to the list of artists sharing the same Motor-Means pair (Artists Classified by Motor-Means pair p. 39 or by Means-Motor pair p. 47).

SITUATING AN ARTIST NOT FEATURED IN THE STUDY

Proceed through the following four-step process:

1. Collect data on the works and the artist:

– Review the artist's "significant" works (i.e., those works that best demonstrate the diversity and complexity of the artist's practice but which also, and crucially, have been pivotal in gaining recognition);
– Read the detailed descriptions of the works to develop a physical, concrete understanding of them. To this end, favor in situ images (which accurately identify the work's scale and relationship to the surroundings or the visitor) and read the detailed descriptions of the techniques and materials used. Privilege statements and writings by the artists themselves (interviews, recordings, videos, books, articles, etc.) and press releases from their gallery. Consider the titles of the works.

2. Identify the artist's Motor:

Understanding an artist's Motor is about reflecting on what actually prompts them to create as opposed to what one perceives in their works. There are as many possible interpretations of a work of art as there are observers. However, it is possible to identify an artist's Motor, and identifying their Motor provides a general understanding of their work and also facilitates making links with other artists or a particular art movement. The Motor is what drives an artist on a fundamental level. It is the artist's central concern, their initial desire, and not what might develop out of it or what interests them in a peripheral manner.

To identify the Motor:

– Start by analyzing the artist's works: Put yourself in the artist's place rather than that of spectator. To find an artist's Motor (their motivations, their concerns) you need to focus on their intention rather than the works' impact on you. Assimilate the brief definitions of the various Motors and ask yourself the following questions: What is the primary register that seems to interest the artist? Which register do the issues dealt with seem to stem from? Do their works convey an identifiable and predominant area of interest, i.e., perception, the system (society and its codes, politics), narration, play, the self, the body?
– Review the data collected (technical descriptions of the works, the artist's statements, press releases from their gallery, exhibition shots, etc.). Focus on the process through which the artist designs and makes their art, because knowing the origins of a piece helps to understand what is driving the artist.

3. Identify the artist's Means:

— Assimilate the Means definitions;
— Browse the Means chart and ask yourself: What is the consistent feature in the artist's modus operandi and in the material form their works take on (vestige-like aspect, playful or hostile relationship to the visitor, traces of actions, interaction with the surroundings, etc.)?

4. Verify:

To verify the Motor-Means pair you have selected for an artist, refer to the list of artists sorted in ascending order of Motor-Means pairs (see Appendix p. 39). Identify artists sharing the same pair: Are the results coherent? If you are still uncertain, you will need to gather more information on the artist, paying particular attention to their own statements.

SPOTLIGHTING THE SINGULARITY OF AN ART PROCESS

You can use the lists provided in the Appendices to see which artists share the same Motors, the same Means, or the same Motor-Means pairs. Comparing the data in this way makes it easier to both spotlight an artist's singularity or originality and identify its characteristics.

Likewise, you can apply the exercise to yourself once you have identified your own configuration.

You can also use it to bring your own singularity into relief by answering the questions that artists sharing the same Motor-Means pair ask themselves: "How does my area of interest and/or my way of approaching it set me apart from my predecessors or from recognized contemporary artists?"

ALTERNATIVE WAYS OF APPLYING THE RESULTS

The charts and the data provided in the Appendices (lists of artists, statistics charts) can also be used to:

— Identify the major international and French trends from 1987 to 2011;
— Determine the most widespread concerns shared by artists in a given period and, consequently, the major messages they convey;
— Identify the most widespread Means used;
— Discover the directions taken and artistic groupings favored by the different actors of the contemporary art world, i.e., galleries, art centers, curators, institutions, art critics and collectors;
— Identify, using the Motor chart, what drives auteurs or creators who belong to artistic fields in which creation is central, i.e., cinema, music, architecture, etc.

appendices

artist selection criteria

The artist selection criteria used here are meant to be as precise and objective as possible. In addition to a common criteria base, some criteria apply only to international artists or to French artists, respectively.

COMMON CRITERIA BASE FOR SELECTING FRENCH AND INTERNATIONAL ARTISTS

As a general grounding, the selection considers the number of exhibitions in recognized venues over a set period (4 or 7 years).

In order to be included, exhibitions must satisfy the following conditions:

– have taken place during the timeframe covered by the study;
– be solo exhibitions;
– have taken place during the artist's lifetime and less than 25 years after their first solo show as the study is only concerned with artist's who contribute to "the art of the now" and not with artists belonging to *The History of Contemporary Art.*

An artist is only considered part of one or other art scene (i.e., the international or French art scene) if they meet **all** selection criteria for the scene in question.

Note: As prestigious as they may be, participation in the following events, awards and projects (even when participation results in an award) is not taken into account:

– The Venice Biennial, Documenta Kassel, Münster Skulptur Project, Manifesta, Berlin Biennial, Sao Paulo Biennial, Art Basel Statements, Art Basel Miami-Positions, Art Basel Unlimited;
– The Turner Prize, Van Gogh Biennial Award, Hugo Boss Prize, ARCO Award to Young Artists, projects run by prestigious organizations (Artangel, London; West of Rome, Pasadena, California, etc.).

CRITERIA FOR SELECTING INTERNATIONAL ARTISTS

To be considered part of the international art scene the artist will have pursued one of the following trajectories:

– **either, within a 4-year period:**
    – a solo exhibition in an international gallery (see Appendix "selection criteria for international galleries" p. 35),
    – a solo exhibition in the United States if the gallery exhibition took place elsewhere,
    – a solo exhibition in a venue of international standing* (see Appendix "selection criteria for world-class venues" and "main international venues selected" p. 36);

    * cannot be located in the same country as the exhibition in an international gallery (nor in a neighboring country) and cannot be the artist's home country (country of birth or residency). In the case of multiple countries of residency, the most favorable selection data applies.

– **or, within a 7-year period,** three exhibitions in contemporary art museums with at least one located in Europe and one in the United States (see Appendix p. 36).

In this study, to be considered part of the French art scene an artist must either be of French nationality, have been born in France or have lived in France for a period in excess of 15 years.

In addition, they will have had, **within a 7-year period**, one of the following trajectories:

- **either:**
    - a solo exhibition in one of the galleries participating in the FIAC art fair,
    - three solo exhibitions in prestigious French venues (see Appendix "selection criteria for French venues" p. 37) — two in France and the other either in France or a neighboring country;
- **or:** two solo exhibitions in renowned contemporary art museums — one in France and the other either in France or in a neighboring country.

international and French gallery/venue selection criteria

SELECTION CRITERIA FOR INTERNATIONAL GALLERIES

Galleries are selected for each year of the various periods under study. For a given year, a gallery is selected if within that year it met all criteria for participation in art fairs, which are also selected for the year in question.

Below is the list of art fair participation selected for each year (Note: "participation 1", "participation 2", "participation 3" refer to the specific participation required regardless of actual chronological order):

- 1987-1998: participation in ART BASEL or ART CHICAGO;
- 1999-2002: participation in two art fairs:
    - Participation 1: ART BASEL Basel or Miami or ART CHICAGO,
    - Participation 2: one of the following fairs: ART BASEL Basel or Miami, ART CHICAGO, ARMORY SHOW, FIAC, ARCO, ART COLOGNE, ART BRUSSELS, ART FORUM BERLIN;
- 2003-2008: participation in two art fairs:
    - Participation 1: ART BASEL Basel or Miami,
    - Participation 2: one of the following fairs, on a different continent from participation 1: ART BASEL Basel or Miami, ARMORY SHOW, FRIEZE, FIAC, ARCO, ART COLOGNE, ART FORUM BERLIN;
- 2009-2011: participation in three art fairs:
    - Participation 1: ART BASEL Basel or Miami,
    - Participation 2 and 3: one of the following fairs: ART BASEL Basel or Miami, ARMORY SHOW, FRIEZE London or New York, FIAC, ARCO, ART BRUSSELS, ART HONG KONG, ART DUBAI, VIP ART FAIR. In addition, at least one of these (Participation 2 or 3) must be on a different continent than Participation 1.
- 2012-2014: participation in three art fairs:
    - Participation 1: ART BASEL Basel or Miami or Hong Kong
    - Participation 2 and 3: one of the following fairs: ART BASEL Basel or Miami or Hong Kong (ART HK in 2012), FRIEZE London or New York, ARMORY SHOW, FIAC, ARCO, ART BRUSSELS, ART DUBAI, VIP ART FAIR. In addition, at least one of these (Participation 2 or 3) must be on a different continent than Participation 1.

SELECTION CRITERIA FOR WORLD-CLASS VENUES

The venues selected are mainly devoted to contemporary art and:

- have an international outlook: at least one third of the artists they represent are overseas artists, and they use English for venue publicity and communication;
- are primarily located in the major cities of the main Western or emerging countries;
- are "dynamic" (at least three exhibitions per year);
- have a "non-specialized" outlook (not committed to any particular medium of contemporary art): art centers and museums devoted to a particular medium (photography, video, drawing, painting, performance, etc.) are not included here.

Contemporary art museums

AUSTRALIA: National Gallery of Victoria, Melbourne / Queensland Art Gallery, South Brisbane / MCA, Sydney **AUSTRIA:** Museum der Moderne, Salzbourg / MAK: Museum für Angewandte Kunst Museum, Vienna / Essl Museum of Contemporary Art, Vienna / MUMOK Museum, Vienna **BELGIUM:** MuHKA, Museum voor Hedendaagse Kunst, Antwerp / SMAK: the Municipal Museum of Contemporary Art, Ghent **CANADA:** Art Gallery of Ontario, Toronto **CHINA:** Museum of Contemporary Art, Shanghai **DENMARK:** AroS Kunstmuseum, Aarhus / Louisiana Museum of Modern Art, Humlebæk **FINLAND:** Pori Art Museum, Pori / Sara Hildén Art Museum, Tampere **FRANCE:** CAPC Musée d'art contemporain, Bordeaux / Musée d'art contemporain de Lyon / MAM/ARC, Musée d´Art Moderne de la Ville de Paris / Centre Pompidou, Paris **GERMANY:** Hamburger Bahnhof, Berlin / Neue Nationalgalerie, Berlin / Kunsthalle, Bielefeld / Kunstmuseum, Bonn / Museum Ludwig, Cologne / Museum Kunst Palast, Düsseldorf / Kunstsammlung NRW (K20 K21), Düsseldorf / Museum Folkwang, Essen / Museum für Moderne Kunst, Frankfurt / Sprengel Museum, Hanover / Kunsthalle Fridericianum, Kassel / Kunstmuseen, Krefeld / Städtisches Museum Abteiberg, Mönchengladbach / Pinakothek der Modern, Munich / Städtische Galerie im Lenbachhaus, Munich / Museum für Gegenwartskunst, Siegen / The Kunstmuseum, Wolfsburg **GREAT BRITAIN:** The Tate Modern, London **ICELAND:** The Living Art Museum, Reykjavik **ISRAEL:** Herzliya Museum of Art, Tel Aviv **ITALY:** GAMeC, Bergamo / MAMbo, Galleria d'Arte Moderna di Bologna / Museum for Modern and Contemporary Art (Museion), Bolzano / MACRO Museo d'Arte Contemporanea, Rome / Palazzo delle Esposizioni, Rome/ Castello di Rivoli, Turin / Galleria Civica d´Arte Moderna e Contemporanea, Turin **JAPAN:** MOCA, Hiroshima / 21st Century Museum of Contemporary Art, Kanazawa / Benesse House Museum, Naoshima and Teshima / Hara Museum of Contemporary Art, Tokyo / Setagaya Art Museum, Tokyo **LUXEMBOURG:** Musée d'Art Moderne Grand-Duc Jean **MEXICO:** Museo Tamayo Arte Contemporanea, Mexico **NETHERLANDS:** Stedelijk Van Abbemuseum, Eindhoven / De Hallen, Haarlem / Bonnefanten Museum, Maastricht / Museum Boijmans Van Beuningen, Rotterdam / Museum het Domein, Sittard / De Pont museum voor hedendaagse kunst, Tilburg / GEM, Museum voor Actuele Kunst, The Hague **NORWAY:** Astrup Fearnley Museet for Moderne Kunst, Oslo / Museet for samtidskunst, Oslo / Stenersenmuseet, Oslo **POLAND:** Zachęta National Gallery of Art, Warsaw **PORTUGAL:** Museu de Arte Contemporanea de Serralves, Porto **RUSSIA:** Moscow Museum of Modern Art, Moscow **SLOVENIA:** Moderna galerija, Ljubljana **SPAIN:** MACBA, Barcelona / MUSAC, Léon, Museo Nacional Centro de Arte Reina Sofía, Madrid **SWEDEN:** Moderna Museet, Stockholm / Bildmuseet, Umeå University's museum, Umeå **SWITZERLAND:** Museum für Gegenwartskunst - Emanuel Hoffmann-Stiftung, Basel / Kunstmuseum, Luzern / Kunstmuseum, St. Gallen / Migros Museum, Zürich **UNITED STATES:** MOCA, Tucson, Arizona / The Berkeley Art Museum, California / Orange County Museum of Art, Newport Beach, California / LACMA, Los Angeles, California / UCLA Hammer Museum, Los Angeles, Californie / MCASD, San Diego, California / SFMOMA, San Francisco, California / MCA, Denver, Colorado / Denver Art Museum, Colorado / Wadsworth Atheneum Museum of Modern Art, Hartford, Connecticut / Miami Art Museum, Florida / MOCA: Museum of Contemporary Art, North Miami, Florida / Art Institute, Chicago, Illinois / The Renaissance Society, Chicago, Illinois / UMASS: The University Museum of Contemporary Art, Amherst, Massachusetts / MASS MoCA, North Adams, Massachusetts / The Rose Art Museum of Brandeis University, Waltham, Massachusetts / Davis Museum and Cultural Center, Wellesley, Massachusetts / ICA Institute of Contemporary Art, Boston, Minnesota / Walker Art Center, Minneapolis, Minnesota / Laumeier Sculpture Park, Saint-Louis, Missouri / Contemporary Art Museum St. Louis, Saint Louis, Missouri / Kemper Art Museum, Saint Louis, Missouri / The Hessel Museum of Art, Hudson, New York State / PS1 Contemporary Art Center, Long Island City, New York / The Metropolitan Museum of Art, New York / MOMA, New York / New Museum, New York / Herbert F. Johnson Museum of Art, Ithaca, New York State / MOCA, Cleveland, Ohio / The Fabric Workshop and Museum, Philadelphia, Pennsylvania / ICA, Philadelphia, Pennsylvania / Dallas Museum of Art, Texas / Modern Art Museum, Fort Worth, Texas / Contemporary Arts Museum Houston, Texas / Henry Art Gallery, Seattle, Washington / INOVA, Milwaukee, Wisconsin.

Art centers

AUSTRALIA : IMA: Institute of Modern Art, Brisbane / ACCA, Melbourne / Artspace, Sydney **AUSTRIA:** Kunsthaus, Bregenz / Magazin 4 - Bregenzer Kunstverein, Bregenz / Kunsthaus, Graz / Kunstverein, Graz / OK-Centrum, Linz / Kunsthalle, Vienna / Secession, Vienna **BULGARIA:** The Institute of Contemporary Art, Sofia **CANADA:** Vancouver Art Gallery, British Columbia / Galerie de l'UQAM, Montreal, Quebec / The Power Plant, Toronto **CHINA:** UCCA: Ullens Center for Contemporary Art, Beijing **CZECH REPUBLIC:** The Brno House of Arts, Brno / Rudolfinum Gallery, Prague **DENMARK:** Nikolaj Copenhagen Contemporary Art Center, Copenhague / Brandts, Odense **FINLAND:** MUU Galerie, Helsinki **FRANCE:** Le Consortium, Dijon / Le Magasin Centre National d'Art Contemporain, Grenoble / Le Spot, Le Havre / Villa Arson, Nice / Palais de Tokyo, Paris / Le Grand Café, Saint-Nazaire / Le Creux de l'enfer, Thiers / IAC, Villeurbanne **GERMANY :** Ludwig Forum für Internationale Kunst, Aachen / Kunstverein, Aachen / Kunstverein, Arnsberg / DAAD Galerie, Berlin / Haus der Kultur der Welt, Berlin / Künstlerhaus Bethanien, Berlin / KW, Berlin / Kunstverein, Bielefeld / Kunsteverein, Bonn / Gesellschaft für Aktuelle Kunst, Bremen / Kunstverein für die Rheinlande und Westfalen, Düsseldorf / Portikus, Frankfurt / Kunsteverein, Frankfurt / Schirn Kunsthalle, Frankfurt / Kunstverein, Freiburg / Deichtorhallen, Hamburg / Kunstverein, Hamburg / Kestnergesellschaft, Hanover / ZKM: Center for Art and Media, Karlsruhe / Kunsthalle, Kiel / Galerie für Zeitgenössische Kunst, Leipzig / Kunsthalle,

Mannheim / Kunstverein, Munich / Kunsthalle, Nuremberg / Künstlerhaus, Stuttgart **GREAT BRITAIN:** Ikon Gallery, Birmingham, England / Arnolfini, Bristol, England / Baltic Center for Contemporary Art, Gateshead, England / Hayward Gallery, London / ICA, London, England / Serpentine Gallery, London, England / Camden Arts Center, London, England / Whitechapel Art Gallery, London, England / Parasol Unit, London, England / Chisenhale Gallery, London, England / Barbican Art Gallery, London, England / Castlefield Gallery, Manchester, England / Manchester Art Gallery, England / Nottingham Contemporary, England / Modern Art, Oxford, England / Site Gallery, Sheffield, England / Northern Gallery for Contemporary Art, Sunderland, England / Dundee Contemporary Arts, Scotland / Fruitmarket Gallery, Edinburgh, Scotland / Tramway, Glasgow, Scotland / CCA, Glasgow, Scotland / Transmission gallery, Glasgow, Scotland **ITALY:** Viafarini, Milan / Castello di Rivara, Turin / Franco Soffiantino Arte Contemporanea, Turin / Palazzo del papesse, Sienna **JAPAN:** CCA, Kitakyushu **NETHERLANDS:** De Appel, Amsterdam / Stedelijk Museum Bureau Amsterdam – SMBA, Amsterdam / Witte de With Center for Contemporary Art, Rotterdam **NEW ZEALAND:** Artspace, Auckland **NORWAY:** Bergen Kunsthall / The Henie Onstad Art Centre, Høvikodden **POLAND:** Ujazdowski Castle, Varsovie **REPUBLIC OF IRELAND :** Douglas Hyde Gallery, Dublin / The Royal Hibernian Academy, Dublin **SPAIN :** Arts Santa Mònica, Barcelona / Sala Rekalde, Bilbao / La Conservera, Ceuti / La Fábrica, Madrid / CAC, Málaga / DA2 - Domus Artium 2002, Salamanca / CGAC Centro Galego de Arte Contemporánea, Santiago de Compostela / IVAM: Instituto Valenciano de Arte Moderno, Valence **SWEDEN:** Konsthall, Malmö / Rooseum Center for Contemporary Art, Malmö / Tensta Konsthall, Spanga / Bonniers Konsthall, Stockholm / Färgfabriken, Stockholm / Magasin 3, Stockholm / Ynglingagatan 1 & Döbelnsgatan 2, Stockholm / Baltic Art Center, Visby **SWITZERLAND:** Kunsthalle, Basel / Kunsthaus Baselland, Basel / Kunsthalle, Bern / Centre d'Art de Fribourg (Kunsthalle Freiburg) / Centre d'Art Contemporain, Geneva / Kunsthaus, Glarus / Centre d'art Neuchâtel / Kunsthalle, St Gallen / Kunsthalle, Zurich **UNITED STATES:** Henry Moore Institute, Leeds, Alabama / CCA Wattis Institute for Contemporary Arts, San Francisco, California / Yerba Buena Center for the arts, San Francisco, California / Des Moines Art Center, Iowa / MIT List Visual Arts Center, Cambridge, Massachusetts / Midway Contemporary Art, Minneapolis, Minnesota / SITE, Santa Fe, New Mexico / Artists Space, New York / The Swiss Institute, New York / White Columns, New York / The Contemporary art centers, Cincinnati, Ohio / Wexner center for the arts, Columbus, Ohio / Artpace, San Antonio, Texas.

Foundations or collections

BELGIUM : Museum Dhondt-Dhaenens, Deurle **FRANCE:** Fondation Cartier, Paris / Kadist Art Foundation, Paris **GERMANY:** Deutsche Guggenheim, Berlin / Sammlung Goetz, Munich **GREAT BRITAIN:** A Foundation, Liverpool, England / Bloomberg Space, London, England / David Roberts Art Foundation, London, England / Saatchi Gallery, London, England **GREECE:** Deste Foundation, Athens **ITALY:** Trussardi Foundation, Milan / Galleria Civica di Arte Contemporanea, Trento / Fondazione Merz, Turin / Fondazione Sandretto Re Rebaudengo, Turin / Fondazione Bevilacqua La Masa, Venice **NETHERLANDS:** De Vleeshal, Middelburg **SPAIN:** Fundació la Caixa, Barcelona / Espai 13, Joan Miró Foundation, Barcelona / Fundación Telefónica, Madrid **SWEDEN:** The Swedish Contemporary Art Foundation, Stockholm **SWITZERLAND :** Fondation Beyeler, Basel / Schaulager, Basel / Daros Collection, Zurich **UNITED STATES:** Rubell Family Collection, Miami, Florida / Dia Beacon Foundation, New York.

SELECTION CRITERIA FOR FRENCH VENUES

It is more difficult to determine the criteria for French venues than for the international scene due to the sheer number of venues in France actively participating in representing "the art of the now".

The venues ultimately selected are venues which:

- have exhibited a large number of artists represented by the leading French galleries;
- have proven to be springboards for helping artists access these same galleries;
- are frequently mentioned or discussed in certain well-established French contemporary art journals (for instance *Art Press*, *le Journal des Arts*, *Beaux-arts Magazine*, *Mouvement*, etc.);
- are "dynamic" (at least four exhibitions per year).

This study does not provide a list of "actor" venues of the French art scene.

artists classified by motor-means pair

Artist	MT	MN
ALMOND D.	1	2
BUCKINGHAM M.	1	2
HUYGHE P.	1	2
MALJKOVIĆ D.	1	2
SUI-MEI TSE	1	2
MACCHI J.	1	3
ESQUIVIAS P.	1	5
KOESTER J.	1	5
PUGNAIRE & RAFFINI	1	5
DELBECQ M.	1	6
OHANIAN M.	1	6
STARLING S.	1	6
STEVENSON M.	1	6
VONNA MICHELL T.	1	8
AUGUSTE-DORMEUIL R.	1	13
CHAMBAUD É.	1	13
DONNELLY T.	1	13
MAIRE B.	1	13
MANČUŠKA J.	1	13
STRUNZ K.	1	13
HEMPEL L.	1	14
WOLFSON J.	1	14
LOCKHART S.	1	17
CLAERBOUT D.	1	19
DEAN T.	1	19
FORTUNÉ M.	1	19
LEWIS M.	1	19
MOULIN N.	1	21
BARTOLINI M.	2	1
PARDO J.	2	1

Artist	MT	MN
REHBERGER T.	2	1
ACKERMANN F.	2	2
BALLET E.	2	2
ERLICH L.	2	2
LIM W. J.	2	2
MALPHETTES P.	2	2
YASS C.	2	2
HEIN J.	2	3
LAMOUROUX V.	2	3
BULLOCH A.	2	4
DE COCK J.	2	5
TAYLOR A.	2	5
ONDÁK R.	2	7
PREGO S.	2	7
KHEDOORI R.	2	12
FÖRG G.	2	13
GEFFRIAUD M.	2	13
PUTRIH T.	2	13
SIBONY G.	2	13
TUAZON O.	2	13
WERMERS N.	2	13
FRANÇOIS M.	2	15
ORTEGA D.	2	15
BLAIS D.	2	16
CABRITA REIS P.	2	16
ERKMEN A.	2	16
IGLESIAS C.	2	16
HUBBARD & BIRCHLER	2	19
COUTURIER S.	2	21
GURSKY A.	2	21

Artist	MT	MN
HÖFER C.	2	21
MEHRETU J.	2	23
DE ROOIJ (DE RIJKE & DE ROOIJ <2006)	3	1
HORN R.	3	1
JOUMARD V.	3	1
PETITGAND D.	3	1
PFEIFFER P.	3	1
PIPPIN S.	3	1
COLLISHAW M.	3	2
WYN EVANS C.	3	2
DETANICO & LAIN	3	3
FLOYER C.	3	3
LAVIER B.	3	3
UKLANSKI P.	3	3
PINAUD P.	3	5
FLOC'H N.	3	6
PFLUMM D.	3	9
VEILHAN X.	3	9
FRITSCH K.	3	10
HONERT M.	3	10
PARKER C.	3	12
ARNAUD P.-O.	3	13
CAMPBELL D.	3	13
FINLAY I. H.	3	13
GABELLONE G.	3	13
GUYTON W.	3	13
MCELHENY J.	3	13
RICHER E.	3	13
ZARKA R.	3	13
ALMENDRA W.	3	14

Artist	MT	MN
COINDET D.	3	14
DAHLEM B.	3	14
FELDMANN H.-P.	3	14
KELM A.	3	14
WILCOX T. J.	3	14
COLEMAN J.	3	17
FAST O.	3	17
DEMAND T.	3	21
RUFF T.	3	21
STRUTH T.	3	21
WELLING J.	3	21
WILLIAMS C.	3	21
BENZAKEN C.	3	24
COGNÉE P.	3	24
GONZALES W.	3	24
HAVEKOST E.	3	24
PERRAMANT B.	3	24
PHILLIPS R.	3	24
PIFFARETTI B.	3	24
SASNAL W.	3	24
TURSIC & MILLE	3	24
BART C.	4	1
DO ESPERITO SANTO I.	4	1
ELIASSON O.	4	1
CARDIFF J.	4	2
DODGE J.	4	2
FINCH S.	4	2
JANSSENS A. V.	4	2
HÖLLER C.	4	3
LE VA B.	4	5
BALULA D.	4	6
FERNÁNDEZ T.	4	10
STOCKHOLDER J.	4	14

Artist	MT	MN
FIGARELLA D.	4	16
ABTS T.	4	24
FRIZE B.	4	24
LASKER J.	4	24
MARTIN J.	4	24
ZIMMERMAN P.	4	24
CLEGG & GUTTMANN	5	1
GILLICK L.	5	1
LEVINE S.	5	1
MORRIS S.	5	1
ROCKENSCHAUB G.	5	1
SOCIÉTÉ RÉALISTE	5	1
STEINBACH H.	5	1
ZOBERNIG H.	5	1
LUM K.	5	3
SUPERFLEX	5	3
XU ZHEN (MADEIN)	5	3
MECKSEPER J.	5	4
SCHER J.	5	4
SIERRA S.	5	4
ZITTEL A.	5	4
DECLERCQ A.	5	5
DELLER J.	5	5
SMITH J.	5	5
SPAULINGS R.	5	5
SNYDER S.	5	6
BARDIN O.	5	7
FRASER A.	5	8
DENNIS A.	5	11
GUPTA Su.	5	12
CARRON V.	5	13
MCCOLLUM A.	5	13
NELSON M.	5	13

Artist	MT	MN
PERNICE M.	5	13
HAWKINS R.	5	14
OP DE BEECK H.	5	14
WALKER Ke.	5	14
WANG DU	5	14
BÜCHEL C.	5	15
GYGI F.	5	15
ATAMAN K.	5	17
BARTANA Y.	5	17
BYRNE G.	5	17
MIK A.	5	17
MRÉJÈN V.	5	17
SULLIVAN C.	5	17
ZMIJEWSKI A.	5	17
VEZZOLI F.	5	18
JOUVE V.	5	21
SERRALONGUE B.	5	21
BRYCE F.	5	23
HALLEY P.	5	24
LAWLER L.	6	1
PRINA S.	6	1
RUTAULT C.	6	1
MCKENZIE L.	6	2
ARDOUVIN P.	6	3
BÉRARD S.	6	3
CLOSKY C.	6	3
DOLLINGER O.	6	3
ENGRAMER S.	6	3
FONTAINE C.	6	3
FROMENT A.	6	3
HUBAUT J.	6	3
JANKOWSKI C.	6	3
JOSEPH P.	6	3

Artist	MT	MN
LABELLE-ROJOUX A.	6	3
LE CHEVALLIER M.	6	3
PERIGOT A.	6	3
PRÉVIEUX J.	6	3
SLOMINSKI A.	6	3
TURK G.	6	3
WOHNSEIFER J.	6	4
BAGHRICHE F.	6	5
BISMUTH P.	6	5
BUBLEX A.	6	6
ALLORA & CALZADILLA	6	7
GARAICOA C.	6	13
HEROLD G.	6	13
TROCKEL R.	6	13
DION M.	6	14
HARRISON R.	6	14
HOROWITZ J.	6	14
LIGON G.	6	14
PERRY G.	6	14
DURANT S.	6	15
XHAFA S.	6	15
WEST F.	6	16
LARSSON A.	6	19
PETTIBON R.	6	23
JAAR A.	7	2
VON BONIN C.	7	2
GONZALEZ-TORRES F.	7	3
MAREPE	7	3
NEUESCHWANDER R.	7	3
REYES P.	7	3
XU BING	7	6
ARAKAWA E.	7	7
ASSUME VIVID ASTRO POCUS	7	7
TIRAVANIJA R.	7	7
WEERASETHAKUL A.	7	7
KIMSOOJA	7	8
CHEN ZHEN	7	11
HUANG YONG PING	7	13
ROLLINS T. & K.O.S	7	13
BLOCHER S.	7	17
GREEN R.	8	1
THATER D.	8	2
WALKER Ka.	8	2
CUEVAS M.	8	3
PERJOVSCHI D.	8	3
FARRELL M.	8	4
NOLAND C.	8	4
ART ORIENTÉ OBJET	8	5
ATLAS GROUP (WALID RAAD)	8	5
BOWERS A.	8	6
NGUYEN-HATSUSHJBA J.	8	6
PETERMAN D.	8	6
PIPER A.	8	6
BRUGUERA T.	8	7
HANNING J.	8	7
CONVERT P.	8	9
BAJEVIC M.	8	13
ARCENEAUX E.	8	14
HAMMONS D.	8	14
HERNÁNDEZ-DÍEZ J-A.	8	14
LEONARD Z.	8	14
FIUZA-FAUSTINO D.	8	15
MANGLANO-OVALLE I.	8	15
SHONIBARE Y.	8	15
AMER G.	8	16
TOGUO B.	8	16
DOUGLAS S.	8	17
FAROCKI H.	8	17
JACIR E.	8	17
JULIEN I.	8	17
WILSON J. & L.	8	17
DOHERTY W.	8	19
SIMON T.	8	21
MOFFATT T.	8	22
MCGEE B.	9	5
BOCK J.	9	8
CHETWYND S.	9	14
FRIEDMAN T.	9	14
TYSON K.	9	14
YASSEF V.	9	14
FIRMAN D.	9	15
MOUILLÉ T.	9	15
BEN-NER G.	9	18
FURNAS B.	9	24
OCAMPO M.	9	24
ANDY HOPE 1930	10	2
SCHULZE A.	10	3
SÉCHAS A.	10	3
WEBER M.	10	3
SHAW R.	10	11
ALTHOFF K.	10	12
REYNAUD-DEWAR L.	10	12
COOKE N.	10	15
DJURBERG N.	10	15
FEINSTEIN R.	10	15
SCHNITGER L.	10	15
MELGAARD B.	10	16
BEDIA J.	10	24
DE BALINCOURT J.	10	24

Artist	MT	MN
DZAMA M.	11	2
KENTRIDGE W.	11	2
HESS N.	11	14
TODERI G.	11	19
GASKELL A.	11	22
RAUCH N.	11	24
RICHTER D.	11	24
AOSHIMA C.	12	2
BLOOM B.	12	2
DAVID E.	12	2
KILIMNIK K.	12	2
WEKUA A.	12	2
NOTELLET O.	12	3
MONTARON L.	12	6
BRIAND M.	12	7
BRUANT & SPANGARO	12	7
OTHONIEL J.-M.	12	10
ROTH D.	12	12
TOBIAS G. & U.	12	12
MACUGA G.	12	13
NOONAN D.	12	13
OLOWSKA P.	12	13
TIXADOR & POINCHEVAL	12	13
VON BRANDENBURG U.	12	13
ROJAS C.	12	14
TAL R	12	14
KRISTALOVA K.	12	15
DAMASCENO J.	12	16
JUST J.	12	19
STRBA A.	12	19
YANG FUDONG	12	19
RIKA N.	12	22
NORDSTRÖM J.	12	23
TOMASELLI F.	12	23
DAWSON V.	12	24
DOIG P.	12	24
EITEL T.	12	24
ESSENHIGH I.	12	24
MAMMA ANDERSSON K.	12	24
PLESSEN M.	12	24
SUGITO H.	12	24
FISCHER U.	13	3
FLEURY S.	13	3
RHOADES J.	13	4
KOONS J.	13	9
MURAKAMI T.	13	9
DELVOYE W.	13	10
LIESKE D.	13	13
BOSSUT É.	13	14
CURLET F.	13	14
DA CUNHA A.	13	14
DENNY S.	13	14
LECKEY M.	13	14
MERCIER M.	13	14
PEINADO B.	13	14
REYLE A.	13	14
SACHS T.	13	14
SCURTI F.	13	14
DUBOSSARSKY & VINOGRADOV	13	24
COFFIN P.	14	2
ESTÈVE L.	14	2
HODGES J.	14	2
ARCANGEL C.	14	3
CUOGHI R.	14	3
FAUGUET R.	14	3
GELITIN	14	3
PIVI P.	14	3
SOLOMOUKHA K.	14	3
HERRERO F.	14	5
MUNIZ V.	14	6
RHODE R.	14	8
KRISANAMIS U.	14	12
WHITE P.	14	12
BISCH K.	14	13
CALAIS S.	14	13
COLEN D.	14	14
DEWAR & GICQUEL	14	14
HANDFORTH M.	14	14
KURI G.	14	14
LAMBIE J.	14	14
LOS CARPINTEROS	14	14
MAJERUS M.	14	14
MARCLAY C.	14	14
MULLER D.	14	14
PRUITT R.	14	14
SCANLAN J.	14	14
SHEARER S.	14	14
SAILSTORFER M.	14	15
SIGNER R.	14	15
THERRIEN R.	14	15
CRAFT L.	14	16
CAO FEI	14	18
OEHLEN A.	14	24
PITTMAN L.	14	24
GONZALEZ-FOERSTER D.	15	2
GRASSO L.	15	2
GRÉAUD L.	15	2
LAMARCHE B.	15	2
LÉVÊQUE C.	15	2

Artist	MT	MN
MAZIÈRES D.	15	2
PARRENO P.	15	2
BERDAGUER & PÉJUS	15	3
CATTELAN M.	15	3
ELMGREEN & DRAGSET	15	3
HIRST D.	15	10
PERRET M-T.	15	13
TROUVÉ T.	15	13
BOYCE M.	15	14
KUSMIROWSKI R.	15	14
VIOLETTE B.	15	14
WEINSTEIN M.	15	14
CHAN P.	15	15
DAY-JACKSON M.	15	15
RONDINONE U.	15	15
SCHINWALD M.	15	15
ZIPP T.	15	15
HIORNS R.	15	16
BARNEY M.	16	2
CHAPMAN J. & D.	16	4
BLAZY M.	16	7
ALTMEJD D.	16	11
JAMIE C.	16	12
RUBY S.	16	12
SCHÜTTE T.	16	12
AMORALES C.	16	13
CURRY A.	16	13
JOHNSON R.	16	13
MONAHAN M.	16	13
BAUDART É.	16	14
DEROUBAIX D.	16	14
NOBLE & WEBSTER	16	14
ROUSSEAU S.	16	14

Artist	MT	MN
TRECARTIN R.	16	14
WILKES C.	16	14
FARMER G.	16	15
JOO M.	16	15
KALLAT J.	16	15
X BALL B.	16	15
EDMIER K.	16	16
HLOBO N.	16	16
HOLSTAD C.	16	16
MARTIN B.	16	16
VAREJÃO A.	16	16
GALLAGHER E.	16	23
MUTU W.	16	23
VERNA J-L.	16	23
BROWN G.	16	24
MIYAJIMA T.	17	2
SANDISON C.	17	2
HIRSCHHORN T.	17	4
SALOMONE Y.	17	5
ANTONI J.	17	7
TALEC N.	17	7
KOH T.	17	8
MEESE J.	17	8
QIU ZHIJIE	17	8
HUAN Z.	17	9
CAI GUO-QIANG	17	10
DO-HO SUH	17	10
MORI M.	17	10
STERBAK J.	17	11
MANDERS M.	17	13
ABSALON	17	15
ATELIER VAN LIESHOUT	17	15
FABRE J.	17	15

Artist	MT	MN
HYBER F.	17	15
SMITH K.	17	15
LAMBRI L.	17	21
NOBLE P.	17	23
ACKERMANN R.	17	24
THOMAS P.	18	3
EIDE EINARSSON G.	18	4
AI WEIWEI	18	6
ALTHAMER P.	18	7
GUILLEMINOT M.	18	7
LAURETTE M.	18	8
VO D.	18	13
THURNAUER A.	18	14
GEERS K.	18	15
MARGOLLES T.	18	15
NESHAT S.	18	15
APPLEBROOG I.	18	16
LANDAU S.	18	16
LINDER	18	23
SAMBA C.	18	24
WILEY K.	18	24
KABAKOV I. & E.	19	2
KELLEY M.	19	2
SHAW J.	19	2
STARR G.	19	2
BARBIER G.	19	3
BREUNING O.	19	3
GRAHAM R.	19	3
LANDERS S.	19	3
LEE T.	19	3
MORIMURA Y.	19	3
ANTILLE E.	19	6
VAN DER WERVE G.	19	6

Artist	MT	MN	Artist	MT	MN	Artist	MT	MN
ALŸS F.	19	7	ÖĞÜT A.	20	3	BEECROFT V.	21	7
CYTTER K.	19	7	SOLAKOV N.	20	3	ONOFRE J.	21	7
CHANG P.	19	8	FOWLER L.	20	5	SEHGAL T.	21	7
KJARTANSSON R.	19	8	ŠEDÁ K.	20	5	QUINN M.	21	10
LINZY K.	19	8	CALLE S.	20	6	PANCHAL G.	21	11
OPIE J.	19	9	COLLIER A.	20	6	BORLAND C.	21	12
GORDON D.	19	10	DAVEY M.	20	6	CANTOR M.	21	12
BRONSTEIN P.	19	13	GARCIA-TORRES M.	20	6	SONE Y.	21	12
KIPPENBERGER M.	19	13	MAGID J.	20	6	BIRCKEN A.	21	13
BARRÉ V.	19	14	STOLL G.T.	20	6	BORNSTEIN J.	21	13
BLANCKART O.	19	14	COLOMER J.	20	7	HENROT C.	21	13
MILLER J.	19	14	MCQUEEN S.	20	7	MOULÈNE J-L.	21	13
MARSHALL M.	19	15	EMIN T.	20	12	YANG H.	21	13
MUÑOZ J.	19	15	ARANDA J.	20	13	BAECHLER D.	21	14
WARDILL E.	19	15	BERNARDETTE CORPORATION	20	13	BURR T.	21	14
DUNNING J.	19	16	PACI A.	20	13	LEGUILLON P.	21	14
SIMPSON L.	19	17	QUAYTMAN R.H.	20	13	LIDÉN K.	21	14
TANDBERG V.	19	17	STINGEL R.	20	13	MARTIN K.	21	14
WEARING G.	19	17	AHTILA E-L.	20	17	PIERSON J.	21	14
BREITZ C.	19	18	BOUROUISSA M.	20	17	SZE S.	21	14
DELLSPERGER B.	19	18	SORIN P.	20	18	TEMPLETON E.	21	14
LAND P.	19	18	GRAHAM P.	20	21	ABDESSEMED A.	21	15
RUILOVA A.	19	20	DIAO D.	20	24	CRUZVILLEGAS A.	21	15
BELIN V.	19	21	SHAW G.	20	24	ISLAM R.	21	15
NARA Y.	19	23	TATAH D.	20	24	PITOISET É.	21	15
SCHNEIDER A-M.	19	23	GANDER R.	21	2	RAMETTE P.	21	15
FAVRE V.	19	24	LECCIA A.	21	2	SARACENO T.	21	15
PERROT P.	19	24	SALA A.	21	2	SOSNOWSKA M.	21	15
YAN LEI	19	24	PARIS G.	21	3	AUAD T. L.	21	16
CESARCO A.	20	3	SHRIGLEY D.	21	3	BOURSIER-MOUGENOT C.	21	16
CREED M.	20	3	WURM E.	21	3	THAUBERGER A.	21	17
LEVÉ É.	20	3	BILLING J.	21	5	TAYLOR-WOOD S.	21	19
MONK J.	20	3	BOURNIGAULT R.	21	5	CREWDSON G.	21	21

Artist	MT	MN
DICORCIA P.-L.	21	21
MYLAYNE J-L.	21	21
POITEVIN É.	21	21
SEKULA A.	21	21
WALL J.	21	21
BALLEN R.	21	22
CLARK L.	21	22
MIKHAILOV B.	21	22
TELLER J.	21	22
MUNTEAN & ROSENBLUM	21	23
CORPET V.	21	24
AKAKÇE H.	22	2
PHILIPSZ S.	22	2
PLENSA J.	22	2
TICHY J.	22	2
WRIGHT R.	22	2
LERICOLAIS R.	22	5
GRANAT A.	22	6
MIRRA H.	22	6
ASDAM K.	22	7
HOUSHIARY S.	22	10
MUECK R.	22	10
RAY C.	22	10
ROTHSCHILD E.	22	10
CECCHINI L.	22	11
KUITCA G.	22	11
SARMENTO J.	22	11
BALKENHOL S.	22	12
GALLACCIO A.	22	12
BALKA M.	22	13
BUSTAMANTE J.-M.	22	13
DEAN M.	22	13
EPAMINONDA H.	22	13

Artist	MT	MN
GAILLARD C.	22	13
HEFUNA S.	22	13
JENSEN S.	22	13
KIAER I.	22	13
KOSHLIAKOV V.	22	13
LEBLON G.	22	13
LEE BUL	22	13
MARCEL D.	22	13
MOTI M.	22	13
OROZCO G.	22	13
PURYEAR M.	22	13
RAEDECKER M.	22	13
ŠARČEVIĆ B.	22	13
STEWEN D.	22	13
UGLOW A.	22	13
WHITEREAD R.	22	13
BESHTY W.	22	14
BRADLEY S.	22	14
BRADSHAW P.	22	14
DONG S.	22	14
GENZKEN I.	22	14
HERNÁNDEZ D.	22	14
HILDEBRANDT G.	22	14
KOO J-A.	22	14
LOWMAN N.	22	14
PRICE S.	22	14
WOOL C.	22	14
ZHANG ENLI	22	14
ATTIA K.	22	15
GUPTA Sh.	22	15
HATOUM M.	22	15
MORRISON P.	22	15
PIENE C.	22	15

Artist	MT	MN
BRANNON M.	22	16
CABANES D.	22	16
GOBER R.	22	16
LOU L.	22	16
THIDET S.	22	16
KANWAR A.	22	17
AITKEN D.	22	19
HILL G.	22	19
NASHASHIBI R.	22	19
SAMORE S.	22	19
TAN F.	22	19
TYKKÄ S.	22	19
AUDER M.	22	20
CASEBERE J.	22	21
DIJKSTRA R.	22	21
ESSER E.	22	21
FUSS A.	22	21
LESUEUR N.	22	21
STREULI B.	22	21
SUGIMOTO H.	22	21
TOSANI P.	22	21
TILLMANS W.	22	22
FORD W.	22	23
BLECKNER R.	22	24
BORREMANS M.	22	24
DESGRANDCHAMPS M.	22	24
DUMAS M.	22	24
GALLACE M.	22	24
PEYTON E.	22	24
RIELLY J.	22	24
TAAFFE P.	22	24
TUYMANS L.	22	24
YAN PEI-MING	22	24

Artist	MT	MN
ZHANG XIAOGANG	22	24
LIN M.	23	2
MAYAUX P.	23	3
GROSSE K.	23	5
MARTIN D.	23	8
SCHEIBITZ T.	23	13
LASSRY E.	23	14
HIRAKAWA N.	23	16
NEPOMUCENO M.	23	16
NETO E.	23	16
RIST P.	23	20
VAN LAMSWEERDE I.	23	22
HERRERA A.	23	23
BELL D.	23	24

Artist	MT	MN
BROWN C.	23	24
CURRIN J.	23	24
FENG ZHENGJIE	23	24
HUME G.	23	24
KOLLE R.	23	24
OWENS L.	23	24
RAE F.	23	24
TSCHÄPE J.	23	24
WILLIAMS S.	23	24
YUSKAVAGE L.	23	24
BONVICINI M.	24	4
LUCAS S.	24	4
SCHNEIDER G.	24	4
MCCARTHY P.	24	7

Artist	MT	MN
MAN V.	24	12
OFILI C.	24	12
PARRINO S.	24	13
DE BRUYCKERE B.	24	15
MARCACCIO F.	24	16
MOLINERO A.	24	16
SERRANO A.	24	21
GOLDIN N.	24	22
PENCHRÉAC'H S.	24	24
SAVILLE J.	24	24
SCHUTZ D.	24	24
TYSON N.	24	24

artists classified by means-motor pair

Artist	MT	MN
BARTOLINI M.	2	1
PARDO J.	2	1
REHBERGER T.	2	1
DE ROOIJ (DE RIJKE & DE ROOIJ <2006)	3	1
HORN R.	3	1
JOUMARD V.	3	1
PETITGAND D.	3	1
PFEIFFER P.	3	1
PIPPIN S.	3	1
BART C.	4	1
DO ESPERITO SANTO I.	4	1
ELIASSON O.	4	1
CLEGG & GUTTMANN	5	1
GILLICK L.	5	1
LEVINE S.	5	1
MORRIS S.	5	1
ROCKENSCHAUB G.	5	1
SOCIÉTÉ RÉALISTE	5	1
STEINBACH H.	5	1
ZOBERNIG H.	5	1
LAWLER L.	6	1
PRINA S.	6	1
RUTAULT C.	6	1
GREEN R.	8	1
ALMOND D.	1	2
BUCKINGHAM M.	1	2
HUYGHE P.	1	2
MALJKOVIĆ D.	1	2
SUI-MEI TSE	1	2
ACKERMANN F.	2	2

Artist	MT	MN
BALLET E.	2	2
ERLICH L.	2	2
LIM W. J.	2	2
MALPHETTES P.	2	2
YASS C.	2	2
COLLISHAW M.	3	2
WYN EVANS C.	3	2
CARDIFF J.	4	2
DODGE J.	4	2
FINCH S.	4	2
JANSSENS A. V.	4	2
MCKENZIE L.	6	2
JAAR A.	7	2
VON BONIN C.	7	2
THATER D.	8	2
WALKER Ka.	8	2
ANDY HOPE 1930	10	2
DZAMA M.	11	2
KENTRIDGE W.	11	2
AOSHIMA C.	12	2
BLOOM B.	12	2
DAVID E.	12	2
KILIMNIK K.	12	2
WEKUA A.	12	2
COFFIN P.	14	2
ESTÈVE L.	14	2
HODGES J.	14	2
GONZALEZ-FOERSTER D.	15	2
GRASSO L.	15	2
GRÉAUD L.	15	2

Artist	MT	MN
LAMARCHE B.	15	2
LÉVÊQUE C.	15	2
MAZIÈRES D.	15	2
PARRENO P.	15	2
BARNEY M.	16	2
MIYAJIMA T.	17	2
SANDISON C.	17	2
KABAKOV I. & E.	19	2
KELLEY M.	19	2
SHAW J.	19	2
STARR G.	19	2
GANDER R.	21	2
LECCIA A.	21	2
SALA A.	21	2
AKAKÇE H.	22	2
PHILIPSZ S.	22	2
PLENSA J.	22	2
TICHY J.	22	2
WRIGHT R.	22	2
LIN M.	23	2
MACCHI J.	1	3
HEIN J.	2	3
LAMOUROUX V.	2	3
DETANICO & LAIN	3	3
FLOYER C.	3	3
LAVIER B.	3	3
UKLANSKI P.	3	3
HÖLLER C.	4	3
LUM K.	5	3
SUPERFLEX	5	3

Artist	MT	MN
XU ZHEN (MADEIN)	5	3
ARDOUVIN P.	6	3
BÉRARD S.	6	3
CLOSKY C.	6	3
DOLLINGER O.	6	3
ENGRAMER S.	6	3
FONTAINE C.	6	3
FROMENT A.	6	3
HUBAUT J.	6	3
JANKOWSKI C.	6	3
JOSEPH P.	6	3
LABELLE-ROJOUX A.	6	3
LE CHEVALLIER M.	6	3
PERIGOT A.	6	3
PRÉVIEUX J.	6	3
SLOMINSKI A.	6	3
TURK G.	6	3
GONZALEZ-TORRES F.	7	3
MAREPE	7	3
NEUESCHWANDER R.	7	3
REYES P.	7	3
CUEVAS M.	8	3
PERJOVSCHI D.	8	3
SCHULZE A.	10	3
SÉCHAS A.	10	3
WEBER M.	10	3
NOTELLET O.	12	3
FISCHER U.	13	3
FLEURY S.	13	3
ARCANGEL C.	14	3
CUOGHI R.	14	3
FAUGUET R.	14	3
GELITIN	14	3

Artist	MT	MN
PIVI P.	14	3
SOLOMOUKHA K.	14	3
BERDAGUER & PÉJUS	15	3
CATTELAN M.	15	3
ELMGREEN & DRAGSET	15	3
THOMAS P.	18	3
BARBIER G.	19	3
BREUNING O.	19	3
GRAHAM R.	19	3
LANDERS S.	19	3
LEE T.	19	3
MORIMURA Y.	19	3
CESARCO A.	20	3
CREED M.	20	3
LEVÉ É.	20	3
MONK J.	20	3
ÖĞÜT A.	20	3
SOLAKOV N.	20	3
PARIS G.	21	3
SHRIGLEY D.	21	3
WURM E.	21	3
MAYAUX P.	23	3
BULLOCH A.	2	4
MECKSEPER J.	5	4
SCHER J.	5	4
SIERRA S.	5	4
ZITTEL A.	5	4
WOHNSEIFER J.	6	4
FARRELL M.	8	4
NOLAND C.	8	4
RHOADES J.	13	4
CHAPMAN J. & D.	16	4
HIRSCHHORN T.	17	4

Artist	MT	MN
EIDE EINARSSON G.	18	4
BONVICINI M.	24	4
LUCAS S.	24	4
SCHNEIDER G.	24	4
ESQUIVIAS P.	1	5
KOESTER J.	1	5
PUGNAIRE & RAFFINI	1	5
DE COCK J.	2	5
TAYLOR A.	2	5
PINAUD P.	3	5
LE VA B.	4	5
DECLERCQ A.	5	5
DELLER J.	5	5
SMITH J.	5	5
SPAULINGS R.	5	5
BAGHRICHE F.	6	5
BISMUTH P.	6	5
ART ORIENTÉ OBJET	8	5
ATLAS GROUP (WALID RAAD)	8	5
MCGEE B.	9	5
HERRERO F.	14	5
SALOMONE Y.	17	5
FOWLER L.	20	5
ŠEDÁ K.	20	5
BILLING J.	21	5
BOURNIGAULT R.	21	5
LERICOLAIS R.	22	5
GROSSE K.	23	5
DELBECQ M.	1	6
OHANIAN M.	1	6
STARLING S.	1	6
STEVENSON M.	1	6
FLOC'H N.	3	6

Artist	MT	MN
BALULA D.	4	6
SNYDER S.	5	6
BUBLEX A.	6	6
XU BING	7	6
BOWERS A.	8	6
NGUYEN-HATSUSHJBA J.	8	6
PETERMAN D.	8	6
PIPER A.	8	6
MONTARON L.	12	6
MUNIZ V.	14	6
AI WEIWEI	18	6
ANTILLE E.	19	6
VAN DER WERVE G.	19	6
CALLE S.	20	6
COLLIER A.	20	6
DAVEY M.	20	6
GARCIA-TORRES M.	20	6
MAGID J.	20	6
STOLL G.T.	20	6
GRANAT A.	22	6
MIRRA H.	22	6
ONDÁK R.	2	7
PREGO S.	2	7
BARDIN O.	5	7
ALLORA & CALZADILLA	6	7
ARAKAWA E.	7	7
ASSUME VIVID ASTRO POCUS	7	7
TIRAVANIJA R.	7	7
WEERASETHAKUL A.	7	7
BRUGUERA T.	8	7
HANNING J.	8	7
BRIAND M.	12	7
BRUANT & SPANGARO	12	7

Artist	MT	MN
BLAZY M.	16	7
ANTONI J.	17	7
TALEC N.	17	7
ALTHAMER P.	18	7
GUILLEMINOT M.	18	7
ALŸS F.	19	7
CYTTER K.	19	7
COLOMER J.	20	7
MCQUEEN S.	20	7
BEECROFT V.	21	7
ONOFRE J.	21	7
SEHGAL T.	21	7
ASDAM K.	22	7
MCCARTHY P.	24	7
VONNA MICHELL T.	1	8
FRASER A.	5	8
KIMSOOJA	7	8
BOCK J.	9	8
RHODE R.	14	8
KOH T.	17	8
MEESE J.	17	8
QIU ZHIJIE	17	8
LAURETTE M.	18	8
CHANG P.	19	8
KJARTANSSON R.	19	8
LINZY K.	19	8
MARTIN D.	23	8
PFLUMM D.	3	9
VEILHAN X.	3	9
CONVERT P.	8	9
KOONS J.	13	9
MURAKAMI T.	13	9
HUAN Z.	17	9

Artist	MT	MN
OPIE J.	19	9
FRITSCH K.	3	10
HONERT M.	3	10
FERNÁNDEZ T.	4	10
OTHONIEL J.-M.	12	10
DELVOYE W.	13	10
HIRST D.	15	10
CAI GUO-QIANG	17	10
DO-HO SUH	17	10
MORI M.	17	10
GORDON D.	19	10
QUINN M.	21	10
HOUSHIARY S.	22	10
MUECK R.	22	10
RAY C.	22	10
ROTHSCHILD E.	22	10
DENNIS A.	5	11
CHEN ZHEN	7	11
SHAW R.	10	11
ALTMEJD D.	16	11
STERBAK J.	17	11
PANCHAL G.	21	11
CECCHINI L.	22	11
KUITCA G.	22	11
SARMENTO J.	22	11
KHEDOORI R.	2	12
PARKER C.	3	12
GUPTA Su.	5	12
ALTHOFF K.	10	12
REYNAUD-DEWAR L.	10	12
ROTH D.	12	12
TOBIAS G. & U.	12	12
KRISANAMIS U.	14	12

Artist	MT	MN	Artist	MT	MN	Artist	MT	MN
WHITE P.	14	12	MCCOLLUM A.	5	13	BORNSTEIN J.	21	13
JAMIE C.	16	12	NELSON M.	5	13	HENROT C.	21	13
RUBY S.	16	12	PERNICE M.	5	13	MOULÈNE J.-L.	21	13
SCHÜTTE T.	16	12	GARAICOA C.	6	13	YANG H.	21	13
EMIN T.	20	12	HEROLD G.	6	13	BALKA M.	22	13
BORLAND C.	21	12	TROCKEL R.	6	13	BUSTAMANTE J.-M.	22	13
CANTOR M.	21	12	HUANG YONG PING	7	13	DEAN M.	22	13
SONE Y.	21	12	ROLLINS T. & K.O.S	7	13	EPAMINONDA H.	22	13
BALKENHOL S.	22	12	BAJEVIC M.	8	13	GAILLARD C.	22	13
GALLACCIO A.	22	12	MACUGA G.	12	13	HEFUNA S.	22	13
MAN V.	24	12	NOONAN D.	12	13	JENSEN S.	22	13
OFILI C.	24	12	OLOWSKA P.	12	13	KIAER I.	22	13
AUGUSTE-DORMEUIL R.	1	13	TIXADOR & POINCHEVAL	12	13	KOSHLIAKOV V.	22	13
CHAMBAUD É.	1	13	VON BRANDENBURG U.	12	13	LEBLON G.	22	13
DONNELLY T.	1	13	LIESKE D.	13	13	LEE BUL	22	13
MAIRE B.	1	13	BISCH K.	14	13	MARCEL D.	22	13
MANČUŠKA J.	1	13	CALAIS S.	14	13	MOTI M.	22	13
STRUNZ K.	1	13	PERRET M-T.	15	13	OROZCO G.	22	13
FÖRG G.	2	13	TROUVÉ T.	15	13	PURYEAR M.	22	13
GEFFRIAUD M.	2	13	AMORALES C.	16	13	RAEDECKER M.	22	13
PUTRIH T.	2	13	CURRY A.	16	13	ŠARČEVIĆ B.	22	13
SIBONY G.	2	13	JOHNSON R.	16	13	STEWEN D.	22	13
TUAZON O.	2	13	MONAHAN M.	16	13	UGLOW A.	22	13
WERMERS N.	2	13	MANDERS M.	17	13	WHITEREAD R.	22	13
ARNAUD P.-O.	3	13	VO D.	18	13	SCHEIBITZ T.	23	13
CAMPBELL D.	3	13	BRONSTEIN P.	19	13	PARRINO S.	24	13
FINLAY I. H.	3	13	KIPPENBERGER M.	19	13	HEMPEL L.	1	14
GABELLONE G.	3	13	ARANDA J.	20	13	WOLFSON J.	1	14
GUYTON W.	3	13	BERNARDETTE CORPORATION	20	13	ALMENDRA W.	3	14
MCELHENY J.	3	13	PACI A.	20	13	COINDET D.	3	14
RICHER E.	3	13	QUAYTMAN R.H.	20	13	DAHLEM B.	3	14
ZARKA R.	3	13	STINGEL R.	20	13	FELDMANN H.-P.	3	14
CARRON V.	5	13	BIRCKEN A.	21	13	KELM A.	3	14

Artist	MT	MN	Artist	MT	MN	Artist	MT	MN
WILCOX T. J.	3	14	DEWAR & GICQUEL	14	14	BESHTY W.	22	14
STOCKHOLDER J.	4	14	HANDFORTH M.	14	14	BRADLEY S.	22	14
HAWKINS R.	5	14	KURI G.	14	14	BRADSHAW P.	22	14
OP DE BEECK H.	5	14	LAMBIE J.	14	14	DONG S.	22	14
WALKER Ke.	5	14	LOS CARPINTEROS	14	14	GENZKEN I.	22	14
WANG DU	5	14	MAJERUS M.	14	14	HERNÁNDEZ D.	22	14
DION M.	6	14	MARCLAY C.	14	14	HILDEBRANDT G.	22	14
HARRISON R.	6	14	MULLER D.	14	14	KOO J-A.	22	14
HOROWITZ J.	6	14	PRUITT R.	14	14	LOWMAN N.	22	14
LIGON G.	6	14	SCANLAN J.	14	14	PRICE S.	22	14
PERRY G.	6	14	SHEARER S.	14	14	WOOL C.	22	14
ARCENEAUX E.	8	14	BOYCE M.	15	14	ZHANG ENLI	22	14
HAMMONS D.	8	14	KUSMIROWSKI R.	15	14	LASSRY E.	23	14
HERNÁNDEZ-DÍEZ J-A.	8	14	VIOLETTE B.	15	14	FRANÇOIS M.	2	15
LEONARD Z.	8	14	WEINSTEIN M.	15	14	ORTEGA D.	2	15
CHETWYND S.	9	14	BAUDART É.	16	14	BÜCHEL C.	5	15
FRIEDMAN T.	9	14	DEROUBAIX D.	16	14	GYGI F.	5	15
TYSON K.	9	14	NOBLE & WEBSTER	16	14	DURANT S.	6	15
YASSEF V.	9	14	ROUSSEAU S.	16	14	XHAFA S.	6	15
HESS N.	11	14	TRECARTIN R.	16	14	FIUZA-FAUSTINO D.	8	15
ROJAS C.	12	14	WILKES C.	16	14	MANGLANO-OVALLE I.	8	15
TAL R	12	14	THURNAUER A.	18	14	SHONIBARE Y.	8	15
BOSSUT É.	13	14	BARRÉ V.	19	14	FIRMAN D.	9	15
CURLET F.	13	14	BLANCKART O.	19	14	MOUILLÉ T.	9	15
DA CUNHA A.	13	14	MILLER J.	19	14	COOKE N.	10	15
DENNY S.	13	14	BAECHLER D.	21	14	DJURBERG N.	10	15
LECKEY M.	13	14	BURR T.	21	14	FEINSTEIN R.	10	15
MERCIER M.	13	14	LEGUILLON P.	21	14	SCHNITGER L.	10	15
PEINADO B.	13	14	LIDÉN K.	21	14	KRISTALOVA K.	12	15
REYLE A.	13	14	MARTIN K.	21	14	SAILSTORFER M.	14	15
SACHS T.	13	14	PIERSON J.	21	14	SIGNER R.	14	15
SCURTI F.	13	14	SZE S.	21	14	THERRIEN R.	14	15
COLEN D.	14	14	TEMPLETON E.	21	14	CHAN P.	15	15

Artist	MT	MN	Artist	MT	MN	Artist	MT	MN
DAY-JACKSON M.	15	15	CABRITA REIS P.	2	16	FAST O.	3	17
RONDINONE U.	15	15	ERKMEN A.	2	16	ATAMAN K.	5	17
SCHINWALD M.	15	15	IGLESIAS C.	2	16	BARTANA Y.	5	17
ZIPP T.	15	15	FIGARELLA D.	4	16	BYRNE G.	5	17
FARMER G.	16	15	WEST F.	6	16	MIK A.	5	17
JOO M.	16	15	AMER G.	8	16	MRÉJÈN V.	5	17
KALLAT J.	16	15	TOGUO B.	8	16	SULLIVAN C.	5	17
X BALL B.	16	15	MELGAARD B.	10	16	ZMIJEWSKI A.	5	17
ABSALON	17	15	DAMASCENO J.	12	16	BLOCHER S.	7	17
ATELIER VAN LIESHOUT	17	15	CRAFT L.	14	16	DOUGLAS S.	8	17
FABRE J.	17	15	HIORNS R.	15	16	FAROCKI H.	8	17
HYBER F.	17	15	EDMIER K.	16	16	JACIR E.	8	17
SMITH K.	17	15	HLOBO N.	16	16	JULIEN I.	8	17
GEERS K.	18	15	HOLSTAD C.	16	16	WILSON J. & L.	8	17
MARGOLLES T.	18	15	MARTIN B.	16	16	SIMPSON L.	19	17
NESHAT S.	18	15	VAREJÃO A.	16	16	TANDBERG V.	19	17
MARSHALL M.	19	15	APPLEBROOG I.	18	16	WEARING G.	19	17
MUÑOZ J.	19	15	LANDAU S.	18	16	AHTILA E-L.	20	17
WARDILL E.	19	15	DUNNING J.	19	16	BOUROUISSA M.	20	17
ABDESSEMED A.	21	15	AUAD T. L.	21	16	THAUBERGER A.	21	17
CRUZVILLEGAS A.	21	15	BOURSIER-MOUGENOT C.	21	16	KANWAR A.	22	17
ISLAM R.	21	15	BRANNON M.	22	16	VEZZOLI F.	5	18
PITOISET É.	21	15	CABANES D.	22	16	BEN-NER G.	9	18
RAMETTE P.	21	15	GOBER R.	22	16	CAO FEI	14	18
SARACENO T.	21	15	LOU L.	22	16	BREITZ C.	19	18
SOSNOWSKA M.	21	15	THIDET S.	22	16	DELLSPERGER B.	19	18
ATTIA K.	22	15	HIRAKAWA N.	23	16	LAND P.	19	18
GUPTA Sh.	22	15	NEPOMUCENO M.	23	16	SORIN P.	20	18
HATOUM M.	22	15	NETO E.	23	16	CLAERBOUT D.	1	19
MORRISON P.	22	15	MARCACCIO F.	24	16	DEAN T.	1	19
PIENE C.	22	15	MOLINERO A.	24	16	FORTUNÉ M.	1	19
DE BRUYCKERE B.	24	15	LOCKHART S.	1	17	LEWIS M.	1	19
BLAIS D.	2	16	COLEMAN J.	3	17	HUBBARD & BIRCHLER	2	19

Artist	MT	MN	Artist	MT	MN	Artist	MT	MN
LARSSON A.	6	19	MYLAYNE J-L.	21	21	NARA Y.	19	23
DOHERTY W.	8	19	POITEVIN É.	21	21	SCHNEIDER A-M.	19	23
TODERI G.	11	19	SEKULA A.	21	21	MUNTEAN & ROSENBLUM	21	23
JUST J.	12	19	WALL J.	21	21	FORD W.	22	23
STRBA A.	12	19	CASEBERE J.	22	21	HERRERA A.	23	23
YANG FUDONG	12	19	DIJKSTRA R.	22	21	BENZAKEN C.	3	24
TAYLOR-WOOD S.	21	19	ESSER E.	22	21	COGNÉE P.	3	24
AITKEN D.	22	19	FUSS A.	22	21	GONZALES W.	3	24
HILL G.	22	19	LESUEUR N.	22	21	HAVEKOST E.	3	24
NASHASHIBI R.	22	19	STREULI B.	22	21	PERRAMANT B.	3	24
SAMORE S.	22	19	SUGIMOTO H.	22	21	PHILLIPS R.	3	24
TAN F.	22	19	TOSANI P.	22	21	PIFFARETTI B.	3	24
TYKKÄ S.	22	19	SERRANO A.	24	21	SASNAL W.	3	24
RUILOVA A.	19	20	MOFFATT T.	8	22	TURSIC & MILLE	3	24
AUDER M.	22	20	GASKELL A.	11	22	ABTS T.	4	24
RIST P.	23	20	RIKA N.	12	22	FRIZE B.	4	24
MOULIN N.	1	21	BALLEN R.	21	22	LASKER J.	4	24
COUTURIER S.	2	21	CLARK L.	21	22	MARTIN J.	4	24
GURSKY A.	2	21	MIKHAILOV B.	21	22	ZIMMERMAN P.	4	24
HÖFER C.	2	21	TELLER J.	21	22	HALLEY P.	5	24
DEMAND T.	3	21	TILLMANS W.	22	22	FURNAS B.	9	24
RUFF T.	3	21	VAN LAMSWEERDE I.	23	22	OCAMPO M.	9	24
STRUTH T.	3	21	GOLDIN N.	24	22	BEDIA J.	10	24
WELLING J.	3	21	MEHRETU J.	2	23	DE BALINCOURT J.	10	24
WILLIAMS C.	3	21	BRYCE F.	5	23	RAUCH N.	11	24
JOUVE V.	5	21	PETTIBON R.	6	23	RICHTER D.	11	24
SERRALONGUE B.	5	21	NORDSTRÖM J.	12	23	DAWSON V.	12	24
SIMON T.	8	21	TOMASELLI F.	12	23	DOIG P.	12	24
LAMBRI L.	17	21	GALLAGHER E.	16	23	EITEL T.	12	24
BELIN V.	19	21	MUTU W.	16	23	ESSENHIGH I.	12	24
GRAHAM P.	20	21	VERNA J-L.	16	23	MAMMA ANDERSSON K.	12	24
CREWDSON G.	21	21	NOBLE P.	17	23	PLESSEN M.	12	24
DICORCIA P.-L.	21	21	LINDER	18	23	SUGITO H.	12	24

Artist	MT	MN
DUBOSSARSKY & VINOGRADOV	13	24
OEHLEN A.	14	24
PITTMAN L.	14	24
BROWN G.	16	24
ACKERMANN R.	17	24
SAMBA C.	18	24
WILEY K.	18	24
FAVRE V.	19	24
PERROT P.	19	24
YAN LEI	19	24
DIAO D.	20	24
SHAW G.	20	24
TATAH D.	20	24
CORPET V.	21	24

Artist	MT	MN
BLECKNER R.	22	24
BORREMANS M.	22	24
DESGRANDCHAMPS M.	22	24
DUMAS M.	22	24
GALLACE M.	22	24
PEYTON E.	22	24
RIELLY J.	22	24
TAAFFE P.	22	24
TUYMANS L.	22	24
YAN PEI-MING	22	24
ZHANG XIAOGANG	22	24
BELL D.	23	24
BROWN C.	23	24
CURRIN J.	23	24

Artist	MT	MN
FENG ZHENGJIE	23	24
HUME G.	23	24
KOLLE R.	23	24
OWENS L.	23	24
RAE F.	23	24
TSCHÄPE J.	23	24
WILLIAMS S.	23	24
YUSKAVAGE L.	23	24
PENCHRÉAC'H S.	24	24
SAVILLE J.	24	24
SCHUTZ D.	24	24
TYSON N.	24	24

statistics / artists

MOTORS 1987-1999

UNDERSTANDING 38%	PERCEPTION 18%	LIMITS 6%	TIME	2%
			SPACE	4%
		MECHANISMS 11%	FORMAT TRANSPOSITION	9%
			SENSORY EXPERIENCE	2%
	SOCIETY/CODES 20%	CONDITIONING 12%	MIMESIS	8%
			DERISION	4%
		UNJUST/ EXCLUSIONARY 9%	ACTS OF SHARING	4%
			DENUNCIATION	5%
DOING 15%	NARRATION 4%	GROTESQUE 2%	PARODIC	1%
			DISQUIETING	1%
		DREAMLIKE 3%	DRAMATIC	0%
			POETIC	3%
	PLAY 10%	LIGHT-HEARTED 5%	MARKETING	2%
			DIY	3%
		MORBID 5%	ENVIRONMENTS	2%
			HYBRIDIZATION	3%
EXPERIENCING 47%	SELF 17%	PERSONAL MYTH 8%	METAPHYSICAL PROJECT	6%
			SOCIALLY ENGAGED	2%
		PERSONAL DRAMA 9%	ROLE-PLAY	6%
			FACTUAL NARRATIVE	3%
	BODY 30%	FRAGILITY 22%	STAGING	6%
			AURATIC PRESENCE	16%
		PLEASURE 8%	SENSUALITY	4%
			TRASHINESS	4%

MOTORS 2000-2002

UNDERSTANDING 37%	PERCEPTION 21%	LIMITS 10%	TIME	4%
			SPACE	6%
		MECHANISMS 12%	FORMAT TRANSPOSITION	8%
			SENSORY EXPERIENCE	4%
	SOCIETY/CODES 16%	CONDITIONING 8%	MIMESIS	4%
			DERISION	4%
		UNJUST/ EXCLUSIONARY 8%	ACTS OF SHARING	2%
			DENUNCIATION	6%
DOING 19%	NARRATION 7%	GROTESQUE 3%	PARODIC	2%
			DISQUIETING	1%
		DREAMLIKE 4%	DRAMATIC	2%
			POETIC	3%
	PLAY 12%	LIGHT-HEARTED 6%	MARKETING	3%
			DIY	3%
		MORBID 6%	ENVIRONMENTS	3%
			HYBRIDIZATION	3%
EXPERIENCING 44%	SELF 17%	PERSONAL MYTH 6%	METAPHYSICAL PROJECT	4%
			SOCIALLY ENGAGED	2%
		PERSONAL DRAMA 11%	ROLE-PLAY	8%
			FACTUAL NARRATIVE	3%
	BODY 27%	FRAGILITY 21%	STAGING	6%
			AURATIC PRESENCE	15%
		PLEASURE 6%	SENSUALITY	4%
			TRASHINESS	2%

MEANS 1987-1999

SET 29%	CONTEXTUAL 24%	WORK-ENVIRONMENT RELATIONSHIP 15%	CLINICAL	8%
			DREAMLIKE	7%
		WORK-VISITOR RELATIONSHIP 9%	PLAYFUL	5%
			HOSTILE	4%
	ASSOCIATING AN ACTION 5%	TRACES 3%	REMAINS	2%
			ICONIC	2%
		LIVE 2%	ALLEGORY	2%
			THE INDIVIDUAL	0%
OBJECT 41%	SACRALIZED 14%	TECHNICAL CHARACTER 8%	COLLECTIVE UNCONSCIOUS	2%
			INDIVIDUAL UNCONSCIOUS	5%
		MANUAL PROCESS 6%	METAPHYSICAL DIMENSION	3%
			PAGAN DIMENSION	4%
	HUMAN SCALE 27%	VESTIGE 17%	UTOPIAS	9%
			POP CULTURE	8%
		THREAT/ PROTECTION RELATION 10%	DRAMATIC	6%
			KINESTHETIC	4%
IMAGE 30%	MOVING 7%	MISE-EN-SCENE 3%	DOCUMENTARY-STYLE	2%
			PARODIC	1%
		STATE 4%	SLOW TEMPO	3%
			RAPID TEMPO	1%
	STILL 23%	AUTOMATED INTERMEDIARY 12%	COLD USE	9%
			VISCERAL USE	3%
		HAND-CRAFTED 11%	DRAWING	1%
			PAINTING	10%

MEANS 2000-2002

SET 35%	CONTEXTUAL 26%	WORK-ENVIRONMENT RELATIONSHIP 16%	CLINICAL	5%
			DREAMLIKE	11%
		WORK-VISITOR RELATIONSHIP 10%	PLAYFUL	7%
			HOSTILE	3%
	ASSOCIATING AN ACTION 8%	TRACES 3%	REMAINS	1%
			ICONIC	2%
		LIVE 5%	ALLEGORY	4%
			THE INDIVIDUAL	1%
OBJECT 35%	SACRALIZED 10%	TECHNICAL CHARACTER 6%	COLLECTIVE UNCONSCIOUS	2%
			INDIVIDUAL UNCONSCIOUS	3%
		MANUAL PROCESS 4%	METAPHYSICAL DIMENSION	0%
			PAGAN DIMENSION	4%
	HUMAN SCALE 25%	VESTIGE 12%	UTOPIAS	5%
			POP CULTURE	7%
		THREAT/ PROTECTION RELATION 13%	DRAMATIC	7%
			KINESTHETIC	6%
IMAGE 30%	MOVING 11%	MISE-EN-SCENE 5%	DOCUMENTARY-STYLE	4%
			PARODIC	1%
		STATE 6%	SLOW TEMPO	6%
			RAPID TEMPO	0%
	STILL 19%	AUTOMATED INTERMEDIARY 7%	COLD USE	6%
			VISCERAL USE	2%
		HAND-CRAFTED 12%	DRAWING	2%
			PAINTING	10%

56

MOTORS 2003-2005

Category	Sub	Detail	Item	%
UNDERSTANDING 37%	PERCEPTION 19%	LIMITS 9%	TIME	4%
			SPACE	5%
		MECHANISMS 10%	FORMAT TRANSPOSITION	6%
			SENSORY EXPERIENCE	4%
	SOCIETY/CODES 17%	CONDITIONING 10%	MIMESIS	5%
			DERISION	5%
		UNJUST/ EXCLUSIONARY 8%	ACTS OF SHARING	2%
			DENUNCIATION	6%
DOING 23%	NARRATION 11%	GROTESQUE 3%	PARODIC	2%
			DISQUIETING	1%
		DREAMLIKE 8%	DRAMATIC	2%
			POETIC	6%
	PLAY 12%	LIGHT-HEARTED 6%	MARKETING	3%
			DIY	3%
		MORBID 6%	ENVIRONMENTS	3%
			HYBRIDIZATION	3%
EXPERIENCING 40%	SELF 12%	PERSONAL MYTH 4%	METAPHYSICAL PROJECT	3%
			SOCIALLY ENGAGED	1%
		PERSONAL DRAMA 9%	ROLE-PLAY	6%
			FACTUAL NARRATIVE	3%
	BODY 28%	FRAGILITY 21%	STAGING	8%
			AURATIC PRESENCE	12%
		PLEASURE 7%	SENSUALITY	5%
			TRASHINESS	2%

MOTORS 2006-2008

Category	Sub	Detail	Item	%
UNDERSTANDING 38%	PERCEPTION 18%	LIMITS 11%	TIME	5%
			SPACE	6%
		MECHANISMS 7%	FORMAT TRANSPOSITION	4%
			SENSORY EXPERIENCE	3%
	SOCIETY/CODES 19%	CONDITIONING 11%	MIMESIS	7%
			DERISION	4%
		UNJUST/ EXCLUSIONARY 9%	ACTS OF SHARING	3%
			DENUNCIATION	6%
DOING 27%	NARRATION 12%	GROTESQUE 3%	PARODIC	2%
			DISQUIETING	2%
		DREAMLIKE 8%	DRAMATIC	2%
			POETIC	7%
	PLAY 15%	LIGHT-HEARTED 8%	MARKETING	2%
			DIY	5%
		MORBID 8%	ENVIRONMENTS	4%
			HYBRIDIZATION	4%
EXPERIENCING 36%	SELF 11%	PERSONAL MYTH 4%	METAPHYSICAL PROJECT	3%
			SOCIALLY ENGAGED	1%
		PERSONAL DRAMA 7%	ROLE-PLAY	4%
			FACTUAL NARRATIVE	3%
	BODY 25%	FRAGILITY 20%	STAGING	8%
			AURATIC PRESENCE	12%
		PLEASURE 5%	SENSUALITY	3%
			TRASHINESS	2%

MEANS 2003-2005

Category	Sub	Detail	Item	%
SET 33%	CONTEXTUAL 24%	WORK-ENVIRONMENT RELATIONSHIP 13%	CLINICAL	3%
			DREAMLIKE	11%
		WORK-VISITOR RELATIONSHIP 11%	PLAYFUL	7%
			HOSTILE	3%
	ASSOCIATING AN ACTION 9%	TRACES 4%	REMAINS	1%
			ICONIC	3%
		LIVE 5%	ALLEGORY	3%
			THE INDIVIDUAL	2%
OBJECT 38%	SACRALIZED 9%	TECHNICAL CHARACTER 5%	COLLECTIVE UNCONSCIOUS	1%
			INDIVIDUAL UNCONSCIOUS	3%
		MANUAL PROCESS 4%	METAPHYSICAL DIMENSION	0%
			PAGAN DIMENSION	4%
	HUMAN SCALE 29%	VESTIGE 18%	UTOPIAS	8%
			POP CULTURE	11%
		THREAT/ PROTECTION RELATION 11%	DRAMATIC	6%
			KINESTHETIC	5%
IMAGE 29%	MOVING 10%	MISE-EN-SCENE 6%	DOCUMENTARY-STYLE	5%
			PARODIC	1%
		STATE 4%	SLOW TEMPO	4%
			RAPID TEMPO	0%
	STILL 19%	AUTOMATED INTERMEDIARY 6%	COLD USE	4%
			VISCERAL USE	2%
		HAND-CRAFTED 13%	DRAWING	2%
			PAINTING	11%

MEANS 2006-2008

Category	Sub	Detail	Item	%
SET 36%	CONTEXTUAL 24%	WORK-ENVIRONMENT RELATIONSHIP 14%	CLINICAL	3%
			DREAMLIKE	11%
		WORK-VISITOR RELATIONSHIP 11%	PLAYFUL	8%
			HOSTILE	3%
	ASSOCIATING AN ACTION 12%	TRACES 7%	REMAINS	4%
			ICONIC	3%
		LIVE 6%	ALLEGORY	3%
			THE INDIVIDUAL	3%
OBJECT 38%	SACRALIZED 8%	TECHNICAL CHARACTER 4%	COLLECTIVE UNCONSCIOUS	1%
			INDIVIDUAL UNCONSCIOUS	3%
		MANUAL PROCESS 4%	METAPHYSICAL DIMENSION	1%
			PAGAN DIMENSION	3%
	HUMAN SCALE 30%	VESTIGE 20%	UTOPIAS	8%
			POP CULTURE	13%
		THREAT/ PROTECTION RELATION 9%	DRAMATIC	7%
			KINESTHETIC	3%
IMAGE 26%	MOVING 11%	MISE-EN-SCENE 7%	DOCUMENTARY-STYLE	6%
			PARODIC	1%
		STATE 4%	SLOW TEMPO	4%
			RAPID TEMPO	0%
	STILL 15%	AUTOMATED INTERMEDIARY 3%	COLD USE	2%
			VISCERAL USE	1%
		HAND-CRAFTED 12%	DRAWING	3%
			PAINTING	9%

statistics / international artists

MOTORS 2009-2011

UNDERSTANDING 32%	PERCEPTION 13%	LIMITS 8%	TIME	4%
			SPACE	4%
		MECHANISMS 5%	FORMAT TRANSPOSITION	3%
			SENSORY EXPERIENCE	2%
	SOCIETY/CODES 19%	CONDITIONING 12%	MIMESIS	8%
			DERISION	4%
		UNJUST/ EXCLUSIONARY 7%	ACTS OF SHARING	3%
			DENUNCIATION	4%
DOING 25%	NARRATION 10%	GROTESQUE 3%	PARODIC	1%
			DISQUIETING	2%
		DREAMLIKE 7%	DRAMATIC	1%
			POETIC	6%
	PLAY 15%	LIGHT-HEARTED 6%	MARKETING	1%
			DIY	5%
		MORBID 8%	ENVIRONMENTS	4%
			HYBRIDIZATION	4%
EXPERIENCING 44%	SELF 16%	PERSONAL MYTH 6%	METAPHYSICAL PROJECT	3%
			SOCIALLY ENGAGED	2%
		PERSONAL DRAMA 11%	ROLE-PLAY	4%
			FACTUAL NARRATIVE	7%
	BODY 27%	FRAGILITY 21%	STAGING	9%
			AURATIC PRESENCE	12%
		PLEASURE 6%	SENSUALITY	4%
			TRASHINESS	2%

MEANS 2009-2011

SET 36%	CONTEXTUAL 22%	WORK-ENVIRONMENT RELATIONSHIP 11%	CLINICAL	2%
			DREAMLIKE	9%
		WORK-VISITOR RELATIONSHIP 11%	PLAYFUL	9%
			HOSTILE	2%
	ASSOCIATING AN ACTION 13%	TRACES 7%	REMAINS	3%
			ICONIC	3%
		LIVE 7%	ALLEGORY	4%
			THE INDIVIDUAL	3%
OBJECT 41%	SACRALIZED 5%	TECHNICAL CHARACTER 3%	COLLECTIVE UNCONSCIOUS	0%
			INDIVIDUAL UNCONSCIOUS	2%
		MANUAL PROCESS 2%	METAPHYSICAL DIMENSION	1%
			PAGAN DIMENSION	1%
	HUMAN SCALE 36%	VESTIGE 26%	UTOPIAS	15%
			POP CULTURE	11%
		THREAT/ PROTECTION RELATION 10%	DRAMATIC	7%
			KINESTHETIC	3%
IMAGE 23%	MOVING 9%	MISE-EN-SCENE 6%	DOCUMENTARY-STYLE	5%
			PARODIC	1%
		STATE 3%	SLOW TEMPO	2%
			RAPID TEMPO	1%
	STILL 14%	AUTOMATED INTERMEDIARY 3%	COLD USE	2%
			VISCERAL USE	1%
		HAND-CRAFTED 11%	DRAWING	2%
			PAINTING	8%

MOTORS 1987-2011

UNDERSTANDING 45%	PERCEPTION 24%	LIMITS 10%	TIME	6%
			SPACE	4%
		MECHANISMS 14%	FORMAT TRANSPOSITION	11%
			SENSORY EXPERIENCE	3%
	SOCIETY/CODES 21%	CONDITIONING 16%	MIMESIS	5%
			DERISION	11%
		UNJUST/ EXCLUSIONARY 5%	ACTS OF SHARING	2%
			DENUNCIATION	3%
DOING 24%	NARRATION 7%	GROTESQUE 3%	PARODIC	2%
			DISQUIETING	1%
		DREAMLIKE 4%	DRAMATIC	0%
			POETIC	4%
	PLAY 16%	LIGHT-HEARTED 7%	MARKETING	3%
			DIY	3%
		MORBID 9%	ENVIRONMENTS	6%
			HYBRIDIZATION	3%
EXPERIENCING 32%	SELF 12%	PERSONAL MYTH 4%	METAPHYSICAL PROJECT	2%
			SOCIALLY ENGAGED	2%
		PERSONAL DRAMA 8%	ROLE-PLAY	5%
			FACTUAL NARRATIVE	3%
	BODY 20%	FRAGILITY 17%	STAGING	9%
			AURATIC PRESENCE	7%
		PLEASURE 3%	SENSUALITY	1%
			TRASHINESS	1%

MEANS 1987-2011

SET 45%	CONTEXTUAL 30%	WORK-ENVIRONMENT RELATIONSHIP 11%	CLINICAL	3%
			DREAMLIKE	8%
		WORK-VISITOR RELATIONSHIP 18%	PLAYFUL	17%
			HOSTILE	1%
	ASSOCIATING AN ACTION 16%	TRACES 11%	REMAINS	6%
			ICONIC	5%
		LIVE 5%	ALLEGORY	4%
			THE INDIVIDUAL	1%
OBJECT 35%	SACRALIZED 3%	TECHNICAL CHARACTER 1%	COLLECTIVE UNCONSCIOUS	1%
			INDIVIDUAL UNCONSCIOUS	0%
		MANUAL PROCESS 1%	METAPHYSICAL DIMENSION	1%
			PAGAN DIMENSION	1%
	HUMAN SCALE 32%	VESTIGE 24%	UTOPIAS	12%
			POP CULTURE	12%
		THREAT/ PROTECTION RELATION 8%	DRAMATIC	4%
			KINESTHETIC	4%
IMAGE 20%	MOVING 3%	MISE-EN-SCENE 3%	DOCUMENTARY-STYLE	1%
			PARODIC	1%
		STATE 1%	SLOW TEMPO	1%
			RAPID TEMPO	0%
	STILL 16%	AUTOMATED INTERMEDIARY 5%	COLD USE	5%
			VISCERAL USE	0%
		HAND-CRAFTED 11%	DRAWING	1%
			PAINTING	9%

elements of cognitive psychology

At the root of an artist's drive to create (the Motor) and their modus operandi (the Means) lies a hierarchized set of deep-seated and sometimes unconscious "convictions" that shape their worldview. Each conviction gives rise to a problem that prompts the individual to work towards a desired state (their quest) by adopting a particular kind of solution. This solution is the answer to their iterative query and pertains to the same primordial theme.

VISIBLE ASPECTS					HIDDEN ASPECTS OF THE MOTOR
UNDERSTANDING	PERCEPTION	LIMITS	TIME	1	
			SPACE	2	CONVICTION: Our perception is limited PROBLEM: A feeling of uncertainty QUEST: Omniscience
		MECHANISMS	FORMAT TRANSPOSITION	3	SOLUTION — THE ARTIST'S MESSAGE: Improving perception — Eulogy of discernment QUERY: The objectiveness of our perception of reality PRIMORDIAL THEME: Truth/Essence
			SENSORY EXPERIENCE	4	
	SOCIETY/CODES	CONDITIONING	MIMESIS	5	CONVICTION: We are conditioned by the system PROBLEM: The fear of a loss of freedom QUEST: Freedom
			DERISION	6	SOLUTION — THE ARTIST'S MESSAGE: Breaking free from the system — Eulogy of independence QUERY: The manipulation of our perception of reality PRIMORDIAL THEME: Morality/Virtue
		UNJUST/EXCLUSIONARY	ACTS OF SHARING	7	CONVICTION: The system is unfair PROBLEM: A feeling of injustice QUEST: Justice
			DENUNCIATION	8	SOLUTION — THE ARTIST'S MESSAGE: Fighting the unfairness of the system — Eulogy of revolt QUERY: The domination of inequality PRIMORDIAL THEME: Morality/Virtue
DOING	NARRATION	GROTESQUE	PARODIC	9	
			DISQUIETING	10	
		DREAMLIKE	DRAMATIC	11	
			POETIC	12	CONVICTION: Reality is dull PROBLEM: Fear of boredom QUEST: Stimulation
	PLAY	LIGHT-HEARTED	MARKETING	13	SOLUTION — THE ARTIST'S MESSAGE: Constructing a more exciting reality — Eulogy of creativity QUERY: Escape from everyday life PRIMORDIAL THEME: Otherness/Exoticism
			DIY	14	
		MORBID	ENVIRONMENTS	15	
			HYBRIDIZATION	16	
EXPERIENCING	SELF	PERSONAL MYTH	METAPHYSICAL PROJECT	17	
			SOCIALLY ENGAGED	18	CONVICTION: I have no identity PROBLEM: Fear of being insignificant QUEST: Identity
		PERSONAL DRAMA	ROLE-PLAY	19	SOLUTION — THE ARTIST'S MESSAGE: Being what I value — Eulogy of originality QUERY: The uniqueness of one's existence PRIMORDIAL THEME: Existence
			FACTUAL NARRATIVE	20	
	BODY	FRAGILITY	STAGING	21	CONVICTION: Existence is fragile PROBLEM: A feeling of vulnerability QUEST: Security
			AURATIC PRESENCE	22	SOLUTION — THE ARTIST'S MESSAGE: Magnifying vulnerability — Eulogy of fragility QUERY: The humanness of existence PRIMORDIAL THEME: Existence
		PLEASURE	SENSUALITY	23	CONVICTION: Living is experiencing PROBLEM: A feeling of numbness QUEST: Experience
			TRASHINESS	24	SOLUTION — THE ARTIST'S MESSAGE: Living intensely — Eulogy of emotion QUERY: The physicality of existence PRIMORDIAL THEME: Existence

VISIBLE ASPECTS					HIDDEN ASPECTS OF THE MEANS
SET	CONTEXTUAL	WORK-ENVIRONMENT RELATIONSHIP	CLINICAL	1	CONVICTION: The surrounding context is integral to the artwork
					PROBLEM: Where to situate the beginning of the artwork
					QUEST: The artwork as Indiscernibility
			DREAMLIKE	2	SOLUTION - THE ARTIST'S MESSAGE: Creating indiscernibility — Eulogy of the indivisible/uncircumscribable
					AESTHETIC: Dematerialization
					PRIMORDIAL THEME: Interaction
		WORK-VISITOR RELATIONSHIP	PLAYFUL	3	CONVICTION: The visitor is integral to the artwork
					PROBLEM: How to include the visitor
					QUEST: The artwork as Reaction
			HOSTILE	4	SOLUTION — THE ARTIST'S MESSAGE: Triggering a reaction — Eulogy of dialogue
					AESTHETIC: Exchange
					PRIMORDIAL THEME: Interaction
	ASSOCIATING AN ACTION	TRACES	REMAINS	5	CONVICTION: The artwork results from an action
					PROBLEM: How to show the action in the artwork
					QUEST: The artwork as Capture
			ICONIC	6	SOLUTION — THE ARTIST'S MESSAGE: Capturing the action — Eulogy of the inaccessible
					AESTHETIC: Resurrection
					PRIMORDIAL THEME: Apparition
		LIVE	ALLEGORY	7	CONVICTION: The artwork is an action
					PROBLEM: How to make an action an artwork
					QUEST: The artwork as Event
			THE INDIVIDUAL	8	SOLUTION — THE ARTIST'S MESSAGE: Constructing the event — Eulogy of the moment
					AESTHETIC: Instantaneity
					PRIMORDIAL THEME: Emergence
OBJECT	SACRALIZED	TECHNICAL CHARACTER	COLLECTIVE UNCONSCIOUS	9	CONVICTION: An artwork is sacralized by its technical character
					PROBLEM: What level of technical prowess is required to sacralize an artwork
					QUEST: The artwork as technological Production
			INDIVIDUAL UNCONSCIOUS	10	SOLUTION — THE ARTIST'S MESSAGE: Using technical innovation — Eulogy of perfection
					AESTHETIC: Celebration
					PRIMORDIAL THEME: Transcendence
		MANUAL PROCESS	METAPHYSICAL DIMENSION	11	CONVICTION: An artwork is sacralized through handcrafting
					PROBLEM: Which type of handcrafting is required to sacralize an artwork
					QUEST: The artwork as handcrafted Production
			PAGAN DIMENSION	12	SOLUTION — THE ARTIST'S MESSAGE: Using handcrafting know-how — Eulogy of imperfection
					AESTHETIC: Ritual
					PRIMORDIAL THEME: Transcendence
	HUMAN SCALE	VESTIGE	UTOPIAS	13	CONVICTION: The artwork is a vestige of Man
					PROBLEM: How to make the artwork a vestige
					QUEST: The artwork as Witness
			POP CULTURE	14	SOLUTION — THE ARTIST'S MESSAGE: Making pastness — Eulogy of the abandoned
					AESTHETIC: Memory
					PRIMORDIAL THEME: Loss
		THREAT/ PROTECTION RELATION	DRAMATIC	15	CONVICTION: The artwork creates vulnerability
					PROBLEM: How to "vulnerabilize' the spectator
					QUEST: The artwork as Vulnerabilization
			KINESTHETIC	16	SOLUTION — THE ARTIST'S MESSAGE: Creating a vulnerabilizing force — Eulogy of the dangerous
					AESTHETIC: Danger
					PRIMORDIAL THEME: Threat
IMAGE	MOVING	MISE-EN-SCENE	DOCUMENTARY-STYLE	17	CONVICTION: The artwork is a staging of reality
					PROBLEM: How to stage reality
					QUEST: The artwork as Staging of reality
			PARODIC	18	SOLUTION — THE ARTIST'S MESSAGE: Staging reality — Eulogy of simulacra
					AESTHETIC: Lifelikeness
					PRIMORDIAL THEME: Artifice
		STATE	SLOW TEMPO	19	CONVICTION: The artwork is temporality
					PROBLEM: How to create duration
					QUEST: The artwork as Flux
			RAPID TEMPO	20	SOLUTION — THE ARTIST'S MESSAGE: Creating temporality — Eulogy of the loss of control
					AESTHETIC: Introspection
					PRIMORDIAL THEME: The Self
	STILL	AUTOMATED INTERMEDIARY	COLD USE	21	CONVICTION: The artwork is an indirect process
					PROBLEM: How to make the art-making process indirect
					QUEST: The artwork as Trace
			VISCERAL USE	22	SOLUTION — THE ARTIST'S MESSAGE: Creating a Trace — Eulogy of untraceability
					AESTHETIC: Control
					PRIMORDIAL THEME: The Self
		HAND-CRAFTED	DRAWING	23	CONVICTION: The artwork is a handcrafted process
					PROBLEM: How to make something by hand
					QUEST: The artwork as Uniqueness
			PAINTING	24	SOLUTION — THE ARTIST'S MESSAGE: Leaving a unique trace of one's handcrafting — Eulogy of traceability
					AESTHETIC: Individuality
					PRIMORDIAL THEME: The Self

index of artists

Legend:

MT: Motor code

MN: Means code

SC: Scene

    I: International

    F: French

    IF: International and French

P1, P2, P3, P4, P5: Periods of participation in the International art scene

    P1: 1987–1999

    P2: 2000–2002

    P3: 2003–2005

    P4: 2006–2008

    P5: 2009–2011

As the study considers a single, global period for the French art scene (F-SC) — 1987-2011 — no further specifications have been made for artists on the French art scene.

Motor-Means: Concise form of the Motor and Means.
For an expanded description see the Motor and Means Charts p. 16 and p. 17.

Artist	MT	MN	SC	P1	P2	P3	P4	P5	Motors and Means
ABDESSEMED Adel	21	15	I			3	4	5	Experiencing the fragility of existence through its staging Human-scale object inscribed in a dramatic threat/protection relation
ABSALON	17	15	I	1					Experiencing one's existence by creating a personal myth endowed with a metaphysical project Human-scale object inscribed in a dramatic threat/protection relation
ABTS Tomma	4	24	I				4	5	Understanding the mechanisms of perception through sensory experience Still, handcrafted image — painting type
ACKERMANN Franz	2	2	I		2	3			Understanding the limits of our perception in terms of space Contextual set that establishes a dreamlike relationship with the environment
ACKERMANN Rita	17	24	I		2	3			Experiencing one's existence by creating a personal myth endowed with a metaphysical project Still, handcrafted image — painting type
AHTILA Eija-Liisa	20	17	I		2	3	4	5	Experiencing one's existence via a factual narrative of one's personal drama Moving image with documentary-style mise-en-scene
AI WEIWEI	18	6	I					5	Experiencing one's existence by creating a socially engaged personal myth Set that associates an action with its icon-type traces
AITKEN Doug	22	19	I		2	3	4	5	Experiencing the fragility of existence through auratic presentification Moving image conveying an introspective state through a slow tempo
AKAKÇE Haluk	22	2	I		2	3	4		Experiencing the fragility of existence through auratic presentification Contextual set that establishes a dreamlike relationship with the environment
ALLORA & CALZADILLA	6	7	I				4	5	Understanding society and its codes in order to show their conditioning nature through derision Set centered around a live, allegorical action
ALMENDRA Wilfrid	15	14	F						Creating morbid play through hybridization Human-scale, 'vestige of pop culture'-type object
ALMOND Darren	1	2	I		2	3	4		Understanding the limits of our perception in terms of time Contextual set that establishes a dreamlike relationship with the environment
ALTHAMER Pawel	18	7	I		2				Experiencing one's existence by creating a socially engaged personal myth Set centered around a live, allegorical action
ALTHOFF Kai	10	12	I			3	4		Creating grotesque narratives using the disquieting mode Object sacralized through a manual process, presenting a pagan dimension
ALTMEJD David	16	11	I				4	5	Creating morbid play through hybridization Object sacralized through a manual process, presenting a metaphysical dimension

Artist	MT	MN	SC	P1	P2	P3	P4	P5	Motors and Means
ALŸS Francis	19	7	I		2	3	4	5	Experiencing one's existence via a role-play-type staging of one's personal drama Set centered around a live, allegorical action
AMER Ghada	8	16	I		2	3	4		Understanding society and its codes in order to denounce their unjust and exclusionary nature Human-scale object inscribed in a kinesthetic threat/protection relation
AMORALES Carlos	16	13	I		2	3	4	5	Creating morbid play through hybridization Human-scale, 'vestige of the utopias'-type object
ANDY HOPE 1930	10	2	I					5	Creating grotesque narratives using the disquieting mode Contextual set that establishes a dreamlike relationship with the environment
ANTILLE Emmanuelle	19	6	I			3			Experiencing one's existence via a role-play-type staging of one's personal drama Set that associates an action with its icon-type traces
ANTONI Janine	17	7	I	1		3		5	Experiencing one's existence by creating a personal myth endowed with a metaphysical project Set centered around a live, allegorical action
AOSHIMA Chiho	12	2	I			3	4		Creating dreamlike narratives using the poetic mode Contextual set that establishes a dreamlike relationship with the environment
APPLEBROOG Ida	18	16	I	1					Experiencing one's existence by creating a socially engaged personal myth Human-scale object inscribed in a kinesthetic threat/protection relation
ARAKAWA Ei	7	7	I					5	Understanding society and its codes in order to show their unjust and exclusionary nature through acts of sharing Set centered around a live, allegorical action
ARANDA Julieta	20	13	I					5	Experiencing one's existence via a factual narrative of one's personal drama Human-scale, 'vestige of the utopias'-type object
ARCANGEL Cory	14	3	I				4	5	Creating light-hearted play through DIY-type work Contextual set that establishes a playful relationship with the visitor
ARCENEAUX Edgar	8	14	I					5	Understanding society and its codes in order to denounce their unjust and exclusionary nature Human-scale, 'vestige of pop culture'-type object
ARDOUVIN Pierre	6	3	F						Understanding society and its codes in order to show their conditioning nature through derision Contextual set that establishes a playful relationship with the visitor
ARNAUD Pierre-Olivier	3	13	F						Understanding the mechanisms of perception through format transposition Human-scale, 'vestige of the utopias'-type object
ART ORIENTÉ OBJET	8	5	F						Understanding society and its codes in order to denounce their unjust and exclusionary nature Set that associates an action with its remains-type traces
ASDAM Knut	22	7	I		2	3			Experiencing the fragility of existence through auratic presentification Set centered around a live, allegorical action
ASSUME VIVID ASTRO POCUS	7	7	I				4	5	Understanding society and its codes in order to show their unjust and exclusionary nature through acts of sharing Set centered around a live, allegorical action
ATAMAN Kutlug	5	17	I		2	3	4	5	Understanding society and its codes in order to show their conditioning nature through mimesis Moving image with documentary-style mise-en-scene
ATELIER VAN LIESHOUT	17	15	I	1	2				Experiencing one's existence by creating a personal myth endowed with a metaphysical project Human-scale object inscribed in a dramatic threat/protection relation
ATLAS GROUP (WALID RAAD)	8	5	I				4	5	Understanding society and its codes in order to denounce their unjust and exclusionary nature Set that associates an action with its remains-type traces
ATTIA Kader	22	15	F						Experiencing the fragility of existence through auratic presentification Human-scale object inscribed in a dramatic threat/protection relation
AUAD Tonico Lemos	21	16	I				4		Experiencing the fragility of existence through its staging Human-scale object inscribed in a kinesthetic threat/protection relation
AUDER Michel	22	20	I	1					Experiencing the fragility of existence through auratic presentification Moving image conveying an intoxicated state through a rapid tempo
AUGUSTE-DORMEUIL Renaud	1	13	F						Understanding the limits of our perception in terms of time Human-scale, 'vestige of the utopias'-type object
BAECHLER Donald	21	14	I	1		3			Experiencing the fragility of existence through its staging Human-scale, 'vestige of pop culture'-type object
BAGHRICHE Fayçal	6	5	F						Understanding society and its codes in order to show their conditioning nature through derision Set that associates an action with its remains-type traces
BAJEVIC Maja	8	13	I			3			Understanding society and its codes in order to denounce their unjust and exclusionary nature Human-scale, 'vestige of the utopias'-type object
BALKA Miroslaw	22	13	I	1	2	3	4	5	Experiencing the fragility of existence through auratic presentification Human-scale, 'vestige of the utopias'-type object
BALKENHOL Stephan	22	12	I	1	2	3	4		Experiencing the fragility of existence through auratic presentification Object sacralized through a manual process, presenting a pagan dimension
BALLEN Roger	21	22	I		2	3	4	5	Experiencing the fragility of existence through its staging Still image produced through the "visceral" use of an automated intermediary

Artist	MT	MN	SC	P1	P2	P3	P4	P5	Motors and Means
BALLET Elisabeth	2	2	F						Understanding the limits of our perception in terms of space Contextual set that establishes a dreamlike relationship with the environment
BALULA Davide	4	6	F						Understanding the mechanisms of perception through sensory experience Set that associates an action with its icon-type traces
BARBIER Gilles	19	3	F						Experiencing one's existence via a role-play-type staging of one's personal drama Contextual set that establishes a playful relationship with the visitor
BARDIN Olivier	5	7	F						Understanding society and its codes in order to show their conditioning nature through mimesis Set centered around a live, allegorical action
BARNEY Matthew	16	2	I	1	2	3	4	5	Creating morbid play through hybridization Contextual set that establishes a dreamlike relationship with the environment
BARRÉ Virginie	19	14	F						Experiencing one's existence via a role-play-type staging of one's personal drama Human-scale, 'vestige of pop culture'-type object
BART Cécile	4	1	F						Understanding the mechanisms of perception through sensory experience Contextual set that establishes a clinical relationship with the environment
BARTANA Yael	5	17	I			3	4	5	Understanding society and its codes in order to show their conditioning nature through mimesis Moving image with documentary-style mise-en-scene
BARTOLINI Massimo	2	1	I		2		4	5	Understanding the limits of our perception in terms of space Contextual set that establishes a clinical relationship with the environment
BAUDART Éric	16	14	F						Creating morbid play through hybridization Human-scale, 'vestige of pop culture'-type object
BEDIA José	10	24	I	1	2				Creating grotesque narratives using the disquieting mode Still, handcrafted image — painting type
BEECROFT Vanessa	21	7	I		2	3			Experiencing the fragility of existence through its staging Set centered around a live, allegorical action
BELIN Valérie	19	21	F						Experiencing one's existence via a role-play-type staging of one's personal drama Still image produced through the "cold" use of an automated intermediary
BELL Dirk	23	24	I					5	Physically experiencing sensual pleasure Still, handcrafted image — painting type
BEN-NER Guy	9	18	I				4		Creating grotesque narratives using the parodic mode Moving image with parodic mise-en-scene
BENZAKEN Carole	3	24	F						Understanding the mechanisms of perception through format transposition Still, handcrafted image — painting type
BÉRARD Stéphane	6	3	F						Understanding society and its codes in order to show their conditioning nature through derision Contextual set that establishes a playful relationship with the visitor
BERDAGUER & PÉJUS	15	3	F						Creating morbid play by shaping environments Contextual set that establishes a playful relationship with the visitor
BERNARDETTE CORPORATION	20	13	I					5	Experiencing one's existence via a factual narrative of one's personal drama Human-scale, 'vestige of the utopias'-type object
BESHTY Walead	22	14	I					5	Experiencing the fragility of existence through auratic presentification Human-scale, 'vestige of pop culture'-type object
BILLING Johanna	21	5	I				4		Experiencing the fragility of existence through its staging Set that associates an action with its remains-type traces
BIRCKEN Alexandra	21	13	I					5	Experiencing the fragility of existence through its staging Human-scale, 'vestige of the utopias'-type object
BISCH Karina	14	13	F						Creating light-hearted play through DIY-type work Human-scale, 'vestige of the utopias'-type object
BISMUTH Pierre	6	5	IF				4		Understanding society and its codes in order to show their conditioning nature through derision Set that associates an action with its remains-type traces
BLAIS Dominique	2	16	F						Understanding the limits of our perception in terms of space Human-scale object inscribed in a kinesthetic threat/protection relation
BLANCKART Olivier	19	14	F						Experiencing one's existence via a role-play-type staging of one's personal drama Human-scale, 'vestige of pop culture'-type object
BLAZY Michel	16	7	F						Creating morbid play through hybridization Set centered around a live, allegorical action
BLECKNER Ross	22	24	I	1	2				Experiencing the fragility of existence through auratic presentification Still, handcrafted image — painting type
BLOCHER Sylvie	7	17	F						Understanding society and its codes in order to show their unjust and exclusionary nature through acts of sharing Moving image with documentary-style mise-en-scene
BLOOM Barbara	12	2	I	1					Creating dreamlike narratives using the poetic mode Contextual set that establishes a dreamlike relationship with the environment

Artist	MT	MN	SC	P1	P2	P3	P4	P5	Motors and Means
BOCK John	9	8	I		2	3	4	5	Creating grotesque narratives using the parodic mode Set centered around a live, personal action
BONVICINI Monica	24	4	I			3	4	5	Physically experiencing trashy pleasure Contextual set that establishes a hostile relationship with the visitor
BORLAND Christine	21	12	I	1	2				Experiencing the fragility of existence through its staging Object sacralized through a manual process, presenting a pagan dimension
BORNSTEIN Jennifer	21	13	I					5	Experiencing the fragility of existence through its staging Human-scale, 'vestige of the utopias'-type object
BORREMANS Mickaël	22	24	I			3	4	5	Experiencing the fragility of existence through auratic presentification Still, handcrafted image — painting type
BOSSUT Étienne	13	14	F						Creating light-hearted play using marketing-type forms of communication Human-scale, 'vestige of pop culture'-type object
BOURNIGAULT Rebecca	21	5	F						Experiencing the fragility of existence through its staging Set that associates an action with its remains-type traces
BOUROUISSA Mohamed	20	17	I					5	Experiencing one's existence via a factual narrative of one's personal drama Moving image with documentary-style mise-en-scene
BOURSIER-MOUGENOT Céleste	21	16	IF			3		5	Experiencing the fragility of existence through its staging Human-scale object inscribed in a kinesthetic threat/protection relation
BOWERS Andrea	8	6	I			3	4	5	Understanding society and its codes in order to denounce their unjust and exclusionary nature Set that associates an action with its icon-type traces
BOYCE Martin	15	14	I				4		Creating morbid play by shaping environments Human-scale, 'vestige of pop culture'-type object
BRADLEY Slater	22	14	I					5	Experiencing the fragility of existence through auratic presentification Human-scale, 'vestige of pop culture'-type object
BRADSHAW Philippe	22	14	I			3			Experiencing the fragility of existence through auratic presentification Human-scale, 'vestige of pop culture'-type object
BRANNON Matthew	22	16	I					5	Experiencing the fragility of existence through auratic presentification Human-scale object inscribed in a kinesthetic threat/protection relation
BREITZ Candice	19	18	I		2	3	4	5	Experiencing one's existence via a role-play-type staging of one's personal drama Moving image with parodic mise-en-scene
BREUNING Olaf	19	3	I		2	3	4		Experiencing one's existence via a role-play-type staging of one's personal drama Contextual set that establishes a playful relationship with the visitor
BRIAND Mathieu	12	7	F						Creating dreamlike narratives using the poetic mode Set centered around a live, allegorical action
BRONSTEIN Pablo	19	13	I					5	Experiencing one's existence via a role-play-type staging of one's personal drama Human-scale, 'vestige of the utopias'-type object
BROWN Cecily	23	24	I		2	3	4	5	Physically experiencing sensual pleasure Still, handcrafted image — painting type
BROWN Glenn	16	24	I					5	Creating morbid play through hybridization Still, handcrafted image — painting type
BRUANT & SPANGARO	12	7	F						Creating dreamlike narratives using the poetic mode Set centered around a live, allegorical action
BRUGUERA Tania	8	7	I				4		Understanding society and its codes in order to denounce their unjust and exclusionary nature Set centered around a live, allegorical action
BRYCE Fernando	5	23	I					5	Understanding society and its codes in order to show their conditioning nature through mimesis Still, handcrafted image — drawing type
BUBLEX Alain	6	6	IF			3			Understanding society and its codes in order to show their conditioning nature through derision Set that associates an action with its icon-type traces
BÜCHEL Christoph	5	15	I				4		Understanding society and its codes in order to show their conditioning nature through mimesis Human-scale object inscribed in a dramatic threat/protection relation
BUCKINGHAM Matthew	1	2	I			3	4	5	Understanding the limits of our perception in terms of time Contextual set that establishes a dreamlike relationship with the environment
BULLOCH Angela	2	4	I		2	3			Understanding the limits of our perception in terms of space Contextual set that establishes a hostile relationship with the visitor
BURR Tom	21	14	I				4	5	Experiencing the fragility of existence through its staging Human-scale, 'vestige of pop culture'-type object
BUSTAMANTE Jean-Marc	22	13	I	1	2	3			Experiencing the fragility of existence through auratic presentification Human-scale, 'vestige of the utopias'-type object
BYRNE Gérard	5	17	I				4	5	Understanding society and its codes in order to show their conditioning nature through mimesis Moving image with documentary-style mise-en-scene

Artist	MT	MN	SC	P1	P2	P3	P4	P5	Motors and Means
CABANES Damien	22	16	F						Experiencing the fragility of existence through auratic presentification Human-scale object inscribed in a kinesthetic threat/protection relation
CABRITA REIS Pedro	2	16	I		2	3			Understanding the limits of our perception in terms of space Human-scale object inscribed in a kinesthetic threat/protection relation
CAI GUO-QIANG	17	10	I			3	4	5	Experiencing one's existence by creating a personal myth endowed with a metaphysical project Object sacralized by its technical character and directed towards the individual unconscious
CALAIS Stéphane	14	13	F						Creating light-hearted play through DIY-type work Human-scale, 'vestige of the utopias'-type object
CALLE Sophie	20	6	I	1	2				Experiencing one's existence via a factual narrative of one's personal drama Set that associates an action with its icon-type traces
CAMPBELL Duncan	3	13	I					5	Understanding the mechanisms of perception through format transposition Human-scale, 'vestige of the utopias'-type object
CANTOR Mircea	21	12	I			3	4	5	Experiencing the fragility of existence through its staging Object sacralized through a manual process, presenting a pagan dimension
CAO FEI	14	18	I				4	5	Creating light-hearted play through DIY-type work Moving image with parodic mise-en-scene
CARDIFF Janet	4	2	I		2	3	4	5	Understanding the mechanisms of perception through sensory experience Contextual set that establishes a dreamlike relationship with the environment
CARRON Valentin	5	13	I					5	Understanding society and its codes in order to show their conditioning nature through mimesis Human-scale, 'vestige of the utopias'-type object
CASEBERE James	22	21	I	1					Experiencing the fragility of existence through auratic presentification Still image produced through the "cold" use of an automated intermediary
CATTELAN Maurizio	15	3	I	1	2	3	4	5	Creating morbid play by shaping environments Contextual set that establishes a playful relationship with the visitor
CECCHINI Loris	22	11	I				4		Experiencing the fragility of existence through auratic presentification Object sacralized through a manual process, presenting a metaphysical dimension
CESARCO Alejandro	20	3	I					5	Experiencing one's existence via a factual narrative of one's personal drama Contextual set that establishes a playful relationship with the visitor
CHAMBAUD Étienne	1	13	F						Understanding the limits of our perception in terms of time Human-scale, 'vestige of the utopias'-type object
CHAN Paul	15	15	I				4	5	Creating morbid play by shaping environments Human-scale object inscribed in a dramatic threat/protection relation
CHANG Patty	19	8	I		2		4		Experiencing one's existence via a role-play-type staging of one's personal drama Set centered around a live, personal action
CHAPMAN Jake & Dinos	16	4	I	1			4		Creating morbid play through hybridization Contextual set that establishes a hostile relationship with the visitor
CHEN ZHEN	7	11	I	1					Understanding society and its codes in order to show their unjust and exclusionary nature through acts of sharing Object sacralized through a manual process, presenting a metaphysical dimension
CHETWYND Spartacus	9	14	I			3	4	5	Creating grotesque narratives using the parodic mode Human-scale, 'vestige of pop culture'-type object
CLAERBOUT David	1	19	I		2		4	5	Understanding the limits of our perception in terms of time Moving image conveying an introspective state through a slow tempo
CLARK Larry	21	22	I	1					Experiencing the fragility of existence through its staging Still image produced through the "visceral" use of an automated intermediary
CLEGG & GUTTMANN	5	1	I	1					Understanding society and its codes in order to show their conditioning nature through mimesis Contextual set that establishes a clinical relationship with the environment
CLOSKY Claude	6	3	F						Understanding society and its codes in order to show their conditioning nature through derision Contextual set that establishes a playful relationship with the visitor
COFFIN Peter	14	2	I				4	5	Creating light-hearted play through DIY-type work Contextual set that establishes a dreamlike relationship with the environment
COGNÉE Philippe	22	24	F						Experiencing the fragility of existence through auratic presentification Still, handcrafted image — painting type
COINDET Delphine	15	13	F						Creating morbid play by shaping environments Human-scale, 'vestige of the utopias'-type object
COLEMAN James	3	17	I	1	2				Understanding the mechanisms of perception through format transposition Moving image with documentary-style mise-en-scene
COLEN Dan	14	14	I					5	Creating light-hearted play through DIY-type work Human-scale, 'vestige of pop culture'-type object
COLLIER Anne	20	6	I					5	Experiencing one's existence via a factual narrative of one's personal drama Set that associates an action with its icon-type traces

Artist	MT	MN	SC	P1	P2	P3	P4	P5	Motors and Means
COLLISHAW Mat	3	2	I		2				Understanding the mechanisms of perception through format transposition Contextual set that establishes a dreamlike relationship with the environment
COLOMER Jordi	20	7	I					5	Experiencing one's existence via a factual narrative of one's personal drama Set centered around a live, allegorical action
CONVERT Pascal	8	9	F						Understanding society and its codes in order to denounce their unjust and exclusionary nature Object sacralized by its technical character and directed towards the collective unconscious
COOKE Nigel	10	15	I				4		Creating grotesque narratives using the disquieting mode Human-scale object inscribed in a dramatic threat/protection relation
CORPET Vincent	21	24	F						Experiencing the fragility of existence through its staging Still, handcrafted image — painting type
COUTURIER Stéphane	2	21	F						Understanding the limits of our perception in terms of space Still image produced through the "cold" use of an automated intermediary
CRAFT Liz	14	16	I		2				Creating light-hearted play through DIY-type work Human-scale object inscribed in a kinesthetic threat/protection relation
CREED Martin	20	3	I		2	3	4	5	Experiencing one's existence via a factual narrative of one's personal drama Contextual set that establishes a playful relationship with the visitor
CREWDSON Gregory	21	21	I	1		3	4	5	Experiencing the fragility of existence through its staging Still image produced through the "cold" use of an automated intermediary
CRUZVILLEGAS Abraham	21	15	I					5	Experiencing the fragility of existence through its staging Human-scale object inscribed in a dramatic threat/protection relation
CUEVAS Minerva	8	3	I				4		Understanding society and its codes in order to denounce their unjust and exclusionary nature Contextual set that establishes a playful relationship with the visitor
CUOGHI Roberto	14	3	I				4	5	Creating light-hearted play through DIY-type work Contextual set that establishes a playful relationship with the visitor
CURLET François	13	14	F						Creating light-hearted play using marketing-type forms of communication Human-scale, 'vestige of pop culture'-type object
CURRIN John	23	24	I	1	2	3			Physically experiencing sensual pleasure Still, handcrafted image — painting type
CURRY Aaron	16	13	I					5	Creating morbid play through hybridization Human-scale, 'vestige of the utopias'-type object
CYTTER Keren	19	7	I					5	Experiencing one's existence via a role-play-type staging of one's personal drama Set centered around a live, allegorical action
DA CUNHA Alexandre	13	14	I				4		Creating light-hearted play using marketing-type forms of communication Human-scale, 'vestige of pop culture'-type object
DAHLEM Björn	3	14	I			3			Understanding the mechanisms of perception through format transposition Human-scale, 'vestige of pop culture'-type object
DAMASCENO José	12	16	I			3	4		Creating dreamlike narratives using the poetic mode Human-scale object inscribed in a kinesthetic threat/protection relation
DAVEY Moyra	20	6	I					5	Experiencing one's existence via a factual narrative of one's personal drama Set that associates an action with its icon-type traces
DAVID Enrico	12	2	I				4	5	Creating dreamlike narratives using the poetic mode Contextual set that establishes a dreamlike relationship with the environment
DAWSON Verne	12	24	I		2	3	4	5	Creating dreamlike narratives using the poetic mode Still, handcrafted image — painting type
DAY-JACKSON Matthew	15	15	I				4	5	Creating morbid play by shaping environments Human-scale object inscribed in a dramatic threat/protection relation
DE BALINCOURT Jules	10	24	I					5	Creating grotesque narratives using the disquieting mode Still, handcrafted image — painting type
DE BRUYCKERE Berlinde	24	15	I				4	5	Physically experiencing trashy pleasure Human-scale object inscribed in a dramatic threat/protection relation
DE COCK Jan	2	5	I				4		Understanding the limits of our perception in terms of space Set that associates an action with its remains-type traces
DE ROOIJ (DE RIJKE & DE ROOIJ <2006)	3	1	I		2	3	4	5	Understanding the mechanisms of perception through format transposition Contextual set that establishes a clinical relationship with the environment
DEAN Michael	22	13	I					5	Experiencing the fragility of existence through auratic presentification Human-scale, 'vestige of the utopias'-type object
DEAN Tacita	1	19	I	1	2	3	4	5	Understanding the limits of our perception in terms of time Moving image conveying an introspective state through a slow tempo
DECLERCQ Alain	5	5	F						Understanding society and its codes in order to show their conditioning nature through mimesis Set that associates an action with its remains-type traces

Artist	MT	MN	SC	P1	P2	P3	P4	P5	Motors and Means
DELBECQ Marcelline	1	6	F						Understanding the limits of our perception in terms of time Set that associates an action with its icon-type traces
DELLER Jeremy	5	5	I				4	5	Understanding society and its codes in order to show their conditioning nature through mimesis Set that associates an action with its remains-type traces
DELLSPERGER Brice	19	18	F						Experiencing one's existence via a role-play-type staging of one's personal drama Moving image with parodic mise-en-scene
DELVOYE Wim	13	10	I	1	2	3	4		Creating light-hearted play using marketing-type forms of communication Object sacralized by its technical character and directed towards the individual unconscious
DEMAND Thomas	3	21	I	1	2	3	4	5	Understanding the mechanisms of perception through format transposition Still image produced through the "cold" use of an automated intermediary
DENNIS Adams	5	11	I	1					Understanding society and its codes in order to show their conditioning nature through mimesis Object sacralized through a manual process, presenting a metaphysical dimension
DENNY Simon	13	14	I					5	Creating light-hearted play using marketing-type forms of communication Human-scale, 'vestige of pop culture'-type object
DEROUBAIX Damien	16	14	F						Creating morbid play through hybridization Human-scale, 'vestige of pop culture'-type object
DESGRANDCHAMPS Marc	22	24	F						Experiencing the fragility of existence through auratic presentification Still, handcrafted image — painting type
DETANICO & LAIN	3	3	F						Understanding the mechanisms of perception through format transposition Contextual set that establishes a playful relationship with the visitor
DEWAR & GICQUEL	14	14	F						Creating light-hearted play through DIY-type work Human-scale, 'vestige of pop culture'-type object
DIAO David	20	24	I	1					Experiencing one's existence via a factual narrative of one's personal drama Still, handcrafted image — painting type
DICORCIA Philip-Lorca	21	21	I	1	2	3	4		Experiencing the fragility of existence through its staging Still image produced through the "cold" use of an automated intermediary
DIJKSTRA Rineke	22	21	I		2	3			Experiencing the fragility of existence through auratic presentification Still image produced through the "cold" use of an automated intermediary
DION Mark	6	14	I	1	2	3	4	5	Understanding society and its codes in order to show their conditioning nature through derision Human-scale, 'vestige of pop culture'-type object
DJURBERG Nathalie	10	15	I				4	5	Creating grotesque narratives using the disquieting mode Human-scale object inscribed in a dramatic threat/protection relation
DO ESPERITO SANTO Iran	4	1	I				4		Understanding the mechanisms of perception through sensory experience Contextual set that establishes a clinical relationship with the environment
DODGE Jason	4	2	I		2	3	4	5	Understanding the mechanisms of perception through sensory experience Contextual set that establishes a dreamlike relationship with the environment
DOHERTY Willie	8	19	I	1	2	3			Understanding society and its codes in order to denounce their unjust and exclusionary nature Moving image conveying an introspective state through a slow tempo
DO-HO SUH	17	10	I		2			5	Experiencing one's existence by creating a personal myth endowed with a metaphysical project Object sacralized by its technical character and directed towards the individual unconscious
DOIG Peter	12	24	I	1	2	3	4	5	Creating dreamlike narratives using the poetic mode Still, handcrafted image — painting type
DOLLINGER Olivier	6	3	F						Understanding society and its codes in order to show their conditioning nature through derision Contextual set that establishes a playful relationship with the visitor
DONG Song	22	14	I					5	Experiencing the fragility of existence through auratic presentification Human-scale, 'vestige of pop culture'-type object
DONNELLY Trisha	1	13	I			3	4	5	Understanding the limits of our perception in terms of time Human-scale, 'vestige of the utopias'-type object
DOUGLAS Stan	8	17	I	1	2	3	4		Understanding society and its codes in order to denounce their unjust and exclusionary nature Moving image with documentary-style mise-en-scene
DUBOSSARSKY & VINOGRADOV	13	24	I			3			Creating light-hearted play using marketing-type forms of communication Still, handcrafted image — painting type
DUMAS Marlene	22	24	I	1	2	3	4		Experiencing the fragility of existence through auratic presentification Still, handcrafted image — painting type
DUNNING Jeanne	19	16	I		2				Experiencing one's existence via a role-play-type staging of one's personal drama Human-scale object inscribed in a kinesthetic threat/protection relation
DURANT Sam	6	15	I		2	3			Understanding society and its codes in order to show their conditioning nature through derision Human-scale object inscribed in a dramatic threat/protection relation
DZAMA Marcel	11	2	I			3	4	5	Creating dreamlike narratives using the dramatic mode Contextual set that establishes a dreamlike relationship with the environment

Artist	MT	MN	SC	P1 P2 P3 P4 P5	Motors and Means
EDMIER Keith	16	16	I	1 3	Creating morbid play through hybridization Human-scale object inscribed in a kinesthetic threat/protection relation
EIDE EINARSSON Gardar	18	4	I	4 5	Experiencing one's existence by creating a socially engaged personal myth Contextual set that establishes a hostile relationship with the visitor
EITEL Tim	12	24	I	3	Creating dreamlike narratives using the poetic mode Still, handcrafted image — painting type
ELIASSON Olafur	4	1	I	1 2 3 4 5	Understanding the mechanisms of perception through sensory experience Contextual set that establishes a clinical relationship with the environment
ELMGREEN & DRAGSET	15	3	I	2 3 4	Creating morbid play by shaping environments Contextual set that establishes a playful relationship with the visitor
EMIN Tracey	20	12	I	1 2 3 4 5	Experiencing one's existence via a factual narrative of one's personal drama Object sacralized through a manual process, presenting a pagan dimension
ENGRAMER Sammy	6	3	F		Understanding society and its codes in order to show their conditioning nature through derision Contextual set that establishes a playful relationship with the visitor
EPAMINONDA Haris	22	13	I	5	Experiencing the fragility of existence through auratic presentification Human-scale, 'vestige of the utopias'-type object
ERKMEN Ayse	2	16	I	3	Understanding the limits of our perception in terms of space Human-scale object inscribed in a kinesthetic threat/protection relation
ERLICH Leandro	2	2	I	4 5	Understanding the limits of our perception in terms of space Contextual set that establishes a dreamlike relationship with the environment
ESQUIVIAS Patricia	1	5	I	5	Understanding the limits of our perception in terms of time Set that associates an action with its remains-type traces
ESSENHIGH Inka	12	24	I	3 4	Creating dreamlike narratives using the poetic mode Still, handcrafted image — painting type
ESSER Elger	22	21	I	2	Experiencing the fragility of existence through auratic presentification Still image produced through the "cold" use of an automated intermediary
ESTÈVE Lionel	14	2	I	4	Creating light-hearted play through DIY-type work Contextual set that establishes a dreamlike relationship with the environment
FABRE Jan	17	15	I	1	Experiencing one's existence by creating a personal myth endowed with a metaphysical project Human-scale object inscribed in a dramatic threat/protection relation
FARMER Geoffrey	16	15	I	5	Creating morbid play through hybridization Human-scale object inscribed in a dramatic threat/protection relation
FAROCKI Harun	8	17	I	3 4 5	Understanding society and its codes in order to denounce their unjust and exclusionary nature Moving image with documentary-style mise-en-scene
FARRELL Malachi	8	4	IF	2	Understanding society and its codes in order to denounce their unjust and exclusionary nature Contextual set that establishes a hostile relationship with the visitor
FAST Omer	3	17	I	4 5	Understanding the mechanisms of perception through format transposition Moving image with documentary-style mise-en-scene
FAUGUET Richard	14	3	F		Creating light-hearted play through DIY-type work Contextual set that establishes a playful relationship with the visitor
FAVRE Valérie	19	24	F		Experiencing one's existence via a role-play-type staging of one's personal drama Still, handcrafted image — painting type
FEINSTEIN Rachel	10	15	I	4	Creating grotesque narratives using the disquieting mode Human-scale object inscribed in a dramatic threat/protection relation
FELDMANN Hans-Peter	3	14	I	1	Understanding the mechanisms of perception through format transposition Human-scale, 'vestige of pop culture'-type object
FENG ZHENGJIE	23	24	I	5	Physically experiencing sensual pleasure Still, handcrafted image — painting type
FERNÁNDEZ Teresita	4	10	I	2 3	Understanding the mechanisms of perception through sensory experience Object sacralized by its technical character and directed towards the individual unconscious
FIGARELLA Dominique	4	16	F		Understanding the mechanisms of perception through sensory experience Human-scale object inscribed in a kinesthetic threat/protection relation
FINCH Spencer	4	2	I	2 3 4	Understanding the mechanisms of perception through sensory experience Contextual set that establishes a dreamlike relationship with the environment
FINLAY Ian Hamilton	3	13	I	1	Understanding the mechanisms of perception through format transposition Human-scale, 'vestige of the utopias'-type object
FIRMAN Daniel	9	15	F		Creating grotesque narratives using the parodic mode Human-scale object inscribed in a dramatic threat/protection relation
FISCHER Urs	13	3	I	2 3 4	Creating light-hearted play using marketing-type forms of communication Contextual set that establishes a playful relationship with the visitor

Artist	MT	MN	SC	P1 P2 P3 P4 P5	Motors and Means
FIUZA-FAUSTINO Didier	8	15	F		Understanding society and its codes in order to denounce their unjust and exclusionary nature Human-scale object inscribed in a dramatic threat/protection relation
FLEURY Sylvie	13	3	I	2	Creating light-hearted play using marketing-type forms of communication Contextual set that establishes a playful relationship with the visitor
FLOC'H Nicolas	3	6	F		Understanding the mechanisms of perception through format transposition Set that associates an action with its icon-type traces
FLOYER Ceal	3	3	I	1 2 3 4 5	Understanding the mechanisms of perception through format transposition Contextual set that establishes a playful relationship with the visitor
FONTAINE Claire	6	3	IF	4 5	Understanding society and its codes in order to show their conditioning nature through derision Contextual set that establishes a playful relationship with the visitor
FORD Walton	22	23	I	5	Experiencing the fragility of existence through auratic presentification Still, handcrafted image — drawing type
FÖRG Günther	2	13	I	1	Understanding the limits of our perception in terms of space Human-scale, 'vestige of the utopias'-type object
FORTUNÉ Maïder	1	19	F		Understanding the limits of our perception in terms of time Moving image conveying an introspective state through a slow tempo
FOWLER Luke	20	5	I	4 5	Experiencing one's existence via a factual narrative of one's personal drama Set that associates an action with its remains-type traces
FRANÇOIS Michel	2	15	I	2 3	Understanding the limits of our perception in terms of space Human-scale object inscribed in a dramatic threat/protection relation
FRASER Andrea	5	8	I	3 4	Understanding society and its codes in order to show their conditioning nature through mimesis Set centered around a live, personal action
FRIEDMAN Tom	9	14	I	1 2 3 5	Creating grotesque narratives using the parodic mode Human-scale, 'vestige of pop culture'-type object
FRITSCH Katharina	3	10	I	1	Understanding the mechanisms of perception through format transposition Object sacralized by its technical character and directed towards the individual unconscious
FRIZE Bernard	4	24	IF	2 3	Understanding the mechanisms of perception through sensory experience Still, handcrafted image — painting type
FROMENT Aurélien	6	3	F		Understanding society and its codes in order to show their conditioning nature through derision Contextual set that establishes a playful relationship with the visitor
FURNAS Baranaby	9	24	I	3	Creating grotesque narratives using the parodic mode Still, handcrafted image — painting type
FUSS Adam	22	21	I	3	Experiencing the fragility of existence through auratic presentification Still image produced through the "cold" use of an automated intermediary
GABELLONE Giuseppe	3	13	I	3	Understanding the mechanisms of perception through format transposition Human-scale, 'vestige of the utopias'-type object
GAILLARD Cyprien	22	13	IF	5	Experiencing the fragility of existence through auratic presentification Human-scale, 'vestige of the utopias'-type object
GALLACCIO Anya	22	12	I	1 2 3	Experiencing the fragility of existence through auratic presentification Object sacralized through a manual process, presenting a pagan dimension
GALLACE Maureen	22	24	I	3 4 5	Experiencing the fragility of existence through auratic presentification Still, handcrafted image — painting type
GALLAGHER Ellen	16	23	I	1 2 3 4 5	Creating morbid play through hybridization Still, handcrafted image — drawing type
GANDER Ryan	21	2	I	3 4 5	Experiencing the fragility of existence through its staging Contextual set that establishes a dreamlike relationship with the environment
GARAICOA Carlos	6	13	I	3 4 5	Understanding society and its codes in order to show their conditioning nature through derision Human-scale, 'vestige of the utopias'-type object
GARCIA-TORRES Mario	20	6	I	5	Experiencing one's existence via a factual narrative of one's personal drama Set that associates an action with its icon-type traces
GASKELL Anna	11	22	I	2	Creating dreamlike narratives using the dramatic mode Still image produced through the "visceral" use of an automated intermediary
GEERS Kendell	18	15	I	1 2 3 4	Experiencing one's existence by creating a socially engaged personal myth Human-scale object inscribed in a dramatic threat/protection relation
GEFFRIAUD Mark	2	13	F		Understanding the limits of our perception in terms of space Human-scale, 'vestige of the utopias'-type object
GELITIN	14	3	I	3 4 5	Creating light-hearted play through DIY-type work Contextual set that establishes a playful relationship with the visitor
GENZKEN Isa	22	14	I	1	Experiencing the fragility of existence through auratic presentification Human-scale, 'vestige of pop culture'-type object

Artist	MT	MN	SC	P1 P2 P3 P4 P5	Motors and Means
GILLICK Liam	5	1	I	1 2 3 4 5	Understanding society and its codes in order to show their conditioning nature through mimesis Contextual set that establishes a clinical relationship with the environment
GOBER Robert	22	16	I	1 2 3 4	Experiencing the fragility of existence through auratic presentification Human-scale object inscribed in a kinesthetic threat/protection relation
GOLDIN Nan	24	22	I	1	Physically experiencing trashy pleasure Still image produced through the "visceral" use of an automated intermediary
GONZALES Wayne	3	24	I	5	Understanding the mechanisms of perception through format transposition Still, handcrafted image — painting type
GONZALEZ-FOERSTER Dominique	15	2	IF	5	Creating morbid play by shaping environments Contextual set that establishes a dreamlike relationship with the environment
GONZALEZ-TORRES Felix	7	3	I	1	Understanding society and its codes in order to show their unjust and exclusionary nature through acts of sharing Contextual set that establishes a playful relationship with the visitor
GORDON Douglas	19	10	I	1 2 3 4 5	Experiencing one's existence via a role-play-type staging of one's personal drama Object sacralized by its technical character and directed towards the individual unconscious
GRAHAM Paul	20	21	I	3 4 5	Experiencing one's existence via a factual narrative of one's personal drama Still image produced through the "cold" use of an automated intermediary
GRAHAM Rodney	19	3	I	1 2 3	Experiencing one's existence via a role-play-type staging of one's personal drama Contextual set that establishes a playful relationship with the visitor
GRANAT Amy	22	6	I	4	Experiencing the fragility of existence through auratic presentification Set that associates an action with its icon-type traces
GRASSO Laurent	15	2	F		Creating morbid play by shaping environments Contextual set that establishes a dreamlike relationship with the environment
GRÉAUD Loris	15	2	F		Creating morbid play by shaping environments Contextual set that establishes a dreamlike relationship with the environment
GREEN Renée	8	1	I	1	Understanding society and its codes in order to denounce their unjust and exclusionary nature Contextual set that establishes a clinical relationship with the environment
GROSSE Katharina	23	5	I	2 3 4 5	Physically experiencing sensual pleasure Set that associates an action with its remains-type traces
GUILLEMINOT Marie-Ange	18	7	I	2	Experiencing one's existence by creating a socially engaged personal myth Set centered around a live, allegorical action
GUPTA Shilpa	22	15	I	5	Experiencing the fragility of existence through auratic presentification Human-scale object inscribed in a dramatic threat/protection relation
GUPTA Subodh	5	12	I	4 5	Understanding society and its codes in order to show their conditioning nature through mimesis Object sacralized through a manual process, presenting a pagan dimension
GURSKY Andreas	2	21	I	1 2 3 4 5	Understanding the limits of our perception in terms of space Still image produced through the "cold" use of an automated intermediary
GUYTON Wade	3	13	I	3 4 5	Understanding the mechanisms of perception through format transposition Human-scale, 'vestige of the utopias'-type object
GYGI Fabrice	5	15	I	3	Understanding society and its codes in order to show their conditioning nature through mimesis Human-scale object inscribed in a dramatic threat/protection relation
HALLEY Peter	5	24	I	1	Understanding society and its codes in order to show their conditioning nature through mimesis Still, handcrafted image — painting type
HAMMONS David	8	14	I	1	Understanding society and its codes in order to denounce their unjust and exclusionary nature Human-scale, 'vestige of pop culture'-type object
HANDFORTH Mark	14	14	I	3 4	Creating light-hearted play through DIY-type work Human-scale, 'vestige of pop culture'-type object
HANNING Jens	8	7	I	4	Understanding society and its codes in order to denounce their unjust and exclusionary nature Set centered around a live, allegorical action
HARRISON Rachel	6	14	I	3 4 5	Understanding society and its codes in order to show their conditioning nature through derision Human-scale, 'vestige of pop culture'-type object
HATOUM Mona	22	15	I	1 2 3 4	Experiencing the fragility of existence through auratic presentification Human-scale object inscribed in a dramatic threat/protection relation
HAVEKOST Eberhard	3	24	I	2 3 4	Understanding the mechanisms of perception through format transposition Still, handcrafted image — painting type
HAWKINS Richard	5	14	I	1 2 4	Understanding society and its codes in order to show their conditioning nature through mimesis Human-scale, 'vestige of pop culture'-type object
HEFUNA Susan	22	13	I	5	Experiencing the fragility of existence through auratic presentification Human-scale, 'vestige of the utopias'-type object
HEIN Jeppe	2	3	I	3 4 5	Understanding the limits of our perception in terms of space Contextual set that establishes a playful relationship with the visitor

Artist	MT	MN	SC	P1	P2	P3	P4	P5	Motors and Means
HEMPEL Lothar	1	14	I		2		4		Understanding the limits of our perception in terms of time Human-scale, 'vestige of pop culture'-type object
HENROT Camille	21	13	F						Experiencing the fragility of existence through its staging Human-scale, 'vestige of the utopias'-type object
HERNÁNDEZ Diango	22	14	I					5	Experiencing the fragility of existence through auratic presentification Human-scale, 'vestige of pop culture'-type object
HERNÁNDEZ-DÍEZ José-Antonio	8	14	I		2	3	4		Understanding society and its codes in order to denounce their unjust and exclusionary nature Human-scale, 'vestige of pop culture'-type object
HEROLD Georg	6	13	I	1					Understanding society and its codes in order to show their conditioning nature through derision Human-scale, 'vestige of the utopias'-type object
HERRERA Arturo	23	23	I		2	3	4		Physically experiencing sensual pleasure Still, handcrafted image — drawing type
HERRERO Federico	14	5	I					5	Creating light-hearted play through DIY-type work Set that associates an action with its remains-type traces
HESS Nic	11	14	I			3	4		Creating dreamlike narratives using the dramatic mode Human-scale, 'vestige of pop culture'-type object
HILDEBRANDT Gregor	22	14	I				4		Experiencing the fragility of existence through auratic presentification Human-scale, 'vestige of pop culture'-type object
HILL Gary	22	19	I	1					Experiencing the fragility of existence through auratic presentification Moving image conveying an introspective state through a slow tempo
HIORNS Roger	15	16	I					5	Creating morbid play by shaping environments Human-scale object inscribed in a kinesthetic threat/protection relation
HIRAKAWA Noritoshi	23	16	I	1					Physically experiencing sensual pleasure Human-scale object inscribed in a kinesthetic threat/protection relation
HIRSCHHORN Thomas	17	4	IF	1	2	3	4	5	Experiencing one's existence by creating a personal myth endowed with a metaphysical project Contextual set that establishes a hostile relationship with the visitor
HIRST Damien	15	10	I	1		3	4	5	Creating morbid play by shaping environments Object sacralized by its technical character and directed towards the individual unconscious
HLOBO Nicholas	16	16	I					5	Creating morbid play through hybridization Human-scale object inscribed in a kinesthetic threat/protection relation
HODGES Jim	14	2	I				4	5	Creating light-hearted play through DIY-type work Contextual set that establishes a dreamlike relationship with the environment
HÖFER Candida	2	21	I	1	2				Understanding the limits of our perception in terms of space Still image produced through the "cold" use of an automated intermediary
HÖLLER Carsten	4	3	I		2	3	4	5	Understanding the mechanisms of perception through sensory experience Contextual set that establishes a playful relationship with the visitor
HOLSTAD Christian	16	16	I			3	4		Creating morbid play through hybridization Human-scale object inscribed in a kinesthetic threat/protection relation
HONERT Martin	3	10	I	1					Understanding the mechanisms of perception through format transposition Object sacralized by its technical character and directed towards the individual unconscious
HORN Roni	3	1	I	1					Understanding the mechanisms of perception through format transposition Contextual set that establishes a clinical relationship with the environment
HOROWITZ Jonathan	6	14	I		2			5	Understanding society and its codes in order to show their conditioning nature through derision Human-scale, 'vestige of pop culture'-type object
HOUSHIARY Shirazeh	22	10	I	1	2				Experiencing the fragility of existence through auratic presentification Object sacralized by its technical character and directed towards the individual unconscious
HUAN Zhang	17	9	I		2				Experiencing one's existence by creating a personal myth endowed with a metaphysical project Object sacralized by its technical character and directed towards the collective unconscious
HUANG YONG PING	7	13	IF	1	2	3	4	5	Understanding society and its codes in order to show their unjust and exclusionary nature through acts of sharing Human-scale, 'vestige of the utopias'-type object
HUBAUT Joël	6	3	F						Understanding society and its codes in order to show their conditioning nature through derision Contextual set that establishes a playful relationship with the visitor
HUBBARD & BIRCHLER	2	19	I		2	3	4	5	Understanding the limits of our perception in terms of space Moving image conveying an introspective state through a slow tempo
HUME Gary	23	24	I	1	2	3	4	5	Physically experiencing sensual pleasure Still, handcrafted image — painting type
HUYGHE Pierre	1	2	IF	1	2	3	4		Understanding the limits of our perception in terms of time Contextual set that establishes a dreamlike relationship with the environment
HYBER Fabrice	17	15	IF	1	2				Experiencing one's existence by creating a personal myth endowed with a metaphysical project Human-scale object inscribed in a dramatic threat/protection relation

Artist	MT	MN	SC	P1	P2	P3	P4	P5	Motors and Means
IGLESIAS Cristina	2	16	I	1	2	3	4		Understanding the limits of our perception in terms of space Human-scale object inscribed in a kinesthetic threat/protection relation
ISLAM Runa	21	15	I			3	4	5	Experiencing the fragility of existence through its staging Human-scale object inscribed in a dramatic threat/protection relation
JAAR Alfredo	7	2	I	1	2				Understanding society and its codes in order to show their unjust and exclusionary nature through acts of sharing Contextual set that establishes a dreamlike relationship with the environment
JACIR Emily	8	17	I			3	4		Understanding society and its codes in order to denounce their unjust and exclusionary nature Moving image with documentary-style mise-en-scene
JAMIE Cameron	16	12	I			3			Creating morbid play through hybridization Object sacralized through a manual process, presenting a pagan dimension
JANKOWSKI Christian	6	3	I		2	3	4	5	Understanding society and its codes in order to show their conditioning nature through derision Contextual set that establishes a playful relationship with the visitor
JANSSENS Ann Veronica	4	2	I			3			Understanding the mechanisms of perception through sensory experience Contextual set that establishes a dreamlike relationship with the environment
JENSEN Sergej	22	13	I				4	5	Experiencing the fragility of existence through auratic presentification Human-scale, 'vestige of the utopias'-type object
JOHNSON Rashid	16	13	I					5	Creating morbid play through hybridization Human-scale, 'vestige of the utopias'-type object
JOO Michael	16	15	I		2				Creating morbid play through hybridization Human-scale object inscribed in a dramatic threat/protection relation
JOSEPH Pierre	6	3	F						Understanding society and its codes in order to show their conditioning nature through derision Contextual set that establishes a playful relationship with the visitor
JOUMARD Véronique	3	1	F						Understanding the mechanisms of perception through format transposition Contextual set that establishes a clinical relationship with the environment
JOUVE Valérie	20	21	F						Experiencing one's existence via a factual narrative of one's personal drama Still image produced through the "cold" use of an automated intermediary
JULIEN Isaac	8	17	I		2	3	4	5	Understanding society and its codes in order to denounce their unjust and exclusionary nature Moving image with documentary-style mise-en-scene
JUST Jesper	12	19	I				4	5	Creating dreamlike narratives using the poetic mode Moving image conveying an introspective state through a slow tempo
KABAKOV Ilya & Emilya	19	2	I	1	2	3	4		Experiencing one's existence via a role-play-type staging of one's personal drama Contextual set that establishes a dreamlike relationship with the environment
KALLAT Jitish	16	15	I					5	Creating morbid play through hybridization Human-scale object inscribed in a dramatic threat/protection relation
KANWAR Amar	22	17	I				4	5	Experiencing the fragility of existence through auratic presentification Moving image with documentary-style mise-en-scene
KELLEY Mike	19	2	I	1	2				Experiencing one's existence via a role-play-type staging of one's personal drama Contextual set that establishes a dreamlike relationship with the environment
KELM Annette	3	14	I				4		Understanding the mechanisms of perception through format transposition Human-scale, 'vestige of pop culture'-type object
KENTRIDGE William	11	2	I		2	3	4	5	Creating dreamlike narratives using the dramatic mode Contextual set that establishes a dreamlike relationship with the environment
KHEDOORI Rachel	2	12	I	1	2				Understanding the limits of our perception in terms of space Object sacralized through a manual process, presenting a pagan dimension
KIAER Ian	22	13	I					5	Experiencing the fragility of existence through auratic presentification Human-scale, 'vestige of the utopias'-type object
KILIMNIK Karen	12	2	I	1	2	3	4	5	Creating dreamlike narratives using the poetic mode Contextual set that establishes a dreamlike relationship with the environment
KIMSOOJA	7	8	I		2	3	4	5	Understanding society and its codes in order to show their unjust and exclusionary nature through acts of sharing Set centered around a live, personal action
KIPPENBERGER Martin	19	13	I	1					Experiencing one's existence via a role-play-type staging of one's personal drama Human-scale, 'vestige of the utopias'-type object
KJARTANSSON Ragnar	19	8	I					5	Experiencing one's existence via a role-play-type staging of one's personal drama Set centered around a live, personal action
KOESTER Joachim	1	5	I	1	2		4		Understanding the limits of our perception in terms of time Set that associates an action with its remains-type traces
KOH Terence	17	8	I			3	4	5	Experiencing one's existence by creating a personal myth endowed with a metaphysical project Set centered around a live, personal action
KOLLE Régine	23	24	F						Physically experiencing sensual pleasure Still, handcrafted image — painting type

Artist	MT	MN	SC	P1	P2	P3	P4	P5	Motors and Means
KOO Jeong-A	22	14	IF			3	4	5	Experiencing the fragility of existence through auratic presentification Human-scale, 'vestige of pop culture'-type object
KOONS Jeff	13	9	I	1	2	3			Creating light-hearted play using marketing-type forms of communication Object sacralized by its technical character and directed towards the collective unconscious
KOSHLIAKOV Valery	22	13	I			3			Experiencing the fragility of existence through auratic presentification Human-scale, 'vestige of the utopias'-type object
KRISANAMIS Udomsak	14	12	I	1	2	3			Creating light-hearted play through DIY-type work Object sacralized through a manual process, presenting a pagan dimension
KRISTALOVA Klara	12	15	I					5	Creating dreamlike narratives using the poetic mode Human-scale object inscribed in a dramatic threat/protection relation
KUITCA Guillermo	22	11	I	1					Experiencing the fragility of existence through auratic presentification Object sacralized through a manual process, presenting a metaphysical dimension
KURI Gabriel	14	14	I			3		5	Creating light-hearted play through DIY-type work Human-scale, 'vestige of pop culture'-type object
KUSMIROWSKI Robert	15	14	I			3			Creating morbid play by shaping environments Human-scale, 'vestige of pop culture'-type object
LABELLE-ROJOUX Arnaud	6	3	F						Understanding society and its codes in order to show their conditioning nature through derision Contextual set that establishes a playful relationship with the visitor
LAMARCHE Bertrand	15	2	F						Creating morbid play by shaping environments Contextual set that establishes a dreamlike relationship with the environment
LAMBIE Jim	14	14	I			3	4	5	Creating light-hearted play through DIY-type work Human-scale, 'vestige of pop culture'-type object
LAMBRI Luisa	17	21	I	1					Experiencing one's existence by creating a personal myth endowed with a metaphysical project Still image produced through the "cold" use of an automated intermediary
LAMOUROUX Vincent	2	3	F						Understanding the limits of our perception in terms of space Contextual set that establishes a playful relationship with the visitor
LAND Peter	19	18	I	1	2				Experiencing one's existence via a role-play-type staging of one's personal drama Moving image with parodic mise-en-scene
LANDAU Sigalit	18	16	I					5	Experiencing one's existence by creating a socially engaged personal myth Human-scale object inscribed in a kinesthetic threat/protection relation
LANDERS Sean	19	3	I			3			Experiencing one's existence via a role-play-type staging of one's personal drama Contextual set that establishes a playful relationship with the visitor
LARSSON Annika	6	19	I		2	3			Understanding society and its codes in order to show their conditioning nature through derision Moving image conveying an introspective state through a slow tempo
LASKER Jonathan	4	24	I	1	2	3			Understanding the mechanisms of perception through sensory experience Still, handcrafted image — painting type
LASSRY Elad	23	14	I					5	Physically experiencing sensual pleasure Human-scale, 'vestige of pop culture'-type object
LAURETTE Matthieu	18	8	IF			3			Experiencing one's existence by creating a socially engaged personal myth Set centered around a live, personal action
LAVIER Bertrand	3	3	I	1					Understanding the mechanisms of perception through format transposition Human-scale, 'vestige of pop culture'-type object
LAWLER Louise	6	1	I	1	2				Understanding society and its codes in order to show their conditioning nature through derision Contextual set that establishes a clinical relationship with the environment
LE CHEVALLIER Martin	6	3	F						Understanding society and its codes in order to show their conditioning nature through derision Contextual set that establishes a playful relationship with the visitor
LE VA Barry	4	5	I	1					Understanding the mechanisms of perception through sensory experience Set that associates an action with its remains-type traces
LEBLON Guillaume	22	13	F						Experiencing the fragility of existence through auratic presentification Human-scale, 'vestige of the utopias'-type object
LECCIA Ange	21	2	F						Experiencing the fragility of existence through its staging Contextual set that establishes a dreamlike relationship with the environment
LECKEY Mark	13	14	I			3	4		Creating light-hearted play using marketing-type forms of communication Human-scale, 'vestige of pop culture'-type object
LEE BUL	22	13	I		2	3	4	5	Experiencing the fragility of existence through auratic presentification Human-scale, 'vestige of the utopias'-type object
LEE Tim	19	3	I					5	Experiencing one's existence via a role-play-type staging of one's personal drama Contextual set that establishes a playful relationship with the visitor
LEGUILLON Pierre	21	14	F						Experiencing the fragility of existence through its staging Human-scale, 'vestige of pop culture'-type object

Artist	MT	MN	SC	P1	P2	P3	P4	P5	Motors and Means
LEONARD Zoe	8	14	I	1	2				Understanding society and its codes in order to denounce their unjust and exclusionary nature Human-scale, 'vestige of pop culture'-type object
LERICOLAIS Rainier	22	5	F						Experiencing the fragility of existence through auratic presentification Set that associates an action with its remains-type traces
LESUEUR Natacha	22	21	F						Experiencing the fragility of existence through auratic presentification Still image produced through the "cold" use of an automated intermediary
LEVÉ Édouard	20	3	F						Experiencing one's existence via a factual narrative of one's personal drama Contextual set that establishes a playful relationship with the visitor
LÉVÊQUE Claude	15	2	IF		2				Creating morbid play by shaping environments Contextual set that establishes a dreamlike relationship with the environment
LEVINE Sherrie	5	1	I	1	2				Understanding society and its codes in order to show their conditioning nature through mimesis Contextual set that establishes a clinical relationship with the environment
LEWIS Mark	1	19	I		2	3			Understanding the limits of our perception in terms of time Moving image conveying an introspective state through a slow tempo
LIDÉN Klara	21	14	I				4	5	Experiencing the fragility of existence through its staging Human-scale, 'vestige of pop culture'-type object
LIESKE David	13	13	I					5	Creating light-hearted play using marketing-type forms of communication Human-scale, 'vestige of the utopias'-type object
LIGON Glenn	6	14	I			3	4		Understanding society and its codes in order to show their conditioning nature through derision Human-scale, 'vestige of pop culture'-type object
LIM Won Ju	2	2	I		2	3	4		Understanding the limits of our perception in terms of space Contextual set that establishes a dreamlike relationship with the environment
LIN Michael	23	2	I			3			Physically experiencing sensual pleasure Contextual set that establishes a dreamlike relationship with the environment
LINDER	18	23	I				4		Experiencing one's existence by creating a socially engaged personal myth Still, handcrafted image — drawing type
LINZY Kalup	19	8	I					5	Experiencing one's existence via a role-play-type staging of one's personal drama Set centered around a live, personal action
LOCKHART Sharon	1	17	I	1	2	3	4	5	Understanding the limits of our perception in terms of time Moving image with documentary-style mise-en-scene
LOS CARPINTEROS	14	14	I		2	3			Creating light-hearted play through DIY-type work Human-scale, 'vestige of pop culture'-type object
LOU Liza	22	16	I		2				Experiencing the fragility of existence through auratic presentification Human-scale object inscribed in a kinesthetic threat/protection relation
LOWMAN Nate	22	14	I					5	Experiencing the fragility of existence through auratic presentification Human-scale, 'vestige of pop culture'-type object
LUCAS Sarah	24	4	I	1		3	4		Physically experiencing trashy pleasure Contextual set that establishes a hostile relationship with the visitor
LUM Ken	5	3	I	1	2				Understanding society and its codes in order to show their conditioning nature through mimesis Contextual set that establishes a playful relationship with the visitor
MACCHI Jorge	1	3	I				4	5	Understanding the limits of our perception in terms of time Contextual set that establishes a playful relationship with the visitor
MACUGA Goshka	12	13	I				4	5	Creating dreamlike narratives using the poetic mode Human-scale, 'vestige of the utopias'-type object
MAGID Jill	20	6	I				4	5	Experiencing one's existence via a factual narrative of one's personal drama Set that associates an action with its icon-type traces
MAIRE Benoît	1	13	F						Understanding the limits of our perception in terms of time Human-scale, 'vestige of the utopias'-type object
MAJERUS Michel	14	14	I		2				Creating light-hearted play through DIY-type work Human-scale, 'vestige of pop culture'-type object
MALJKOVIĆ David	1	2	I				4	5	Understanding the limits of our perception in terms of time Contextual set that establishes a dreamlike relationship with the environment
MALPHETTES Pierre	2	2	F						Understanding the limits of our perception in terms of space Contextual set that establishes a dreamlike relationship with the environment
MAMMA ANDERSSON Karin	12	24	I				4		Creating dreamlike narratives using the poetic mode Still, handcrafted image — painting type
MAN Victor	24	12	I					5	Physically experiencing trashy pleasure Object sacralized through a manual process, presenting a pagan dimension
MANČUŠKA Ján	1	13	I					5	Understanding the limits of our perception in terms of time Human-scale, 'vestige of the utopias'-type object

Artist	MT	MN	SC	P1	P2	P3	P4	P5	Motors and Means
MANDERS Mark	17	13	I		2	3	4	5	Experiencing one's existence by creating a personal myth endowed with a metaphysical project Human-scale, 'vestige of the utopias'-type object
MANGLANO-OVALLE Iñigo	8	15	I			3			Understanding society and its codes in order to denounce their unjust and exclusionary nature Human-scale object inscribed in a dramatic threat/protection relation
MARCACCIO Fabian	24	16	I	1	2	3			Physically experiencing trashy pleasure Human-scale object inscribed in a kinesthetic threat/protection relation
MARCEL Didier	22	13	F						Experiencing the fragility of existence through auratic presentification Human-scale, 'vestige of the utopias'-type object
MARCLAY Christian	14	14	I		2	3	4		Creating light-hearted play through DIY-type work Human-scale, 'vestige of pop culture'-type object
MAREPE	7	3	I				4	5	Understanding society and its codes in order to show their unjust and exclusionary nature through acts of sharing Contextual set that establishes a playful relationship with the visitor
MARGOLLES Teresa	18	15	I					5	Experiencing one's existence by creating a socially engaged personal myth Human-scale object inscribed in a dramatic threat/protection relation
MARSHALL Maria	19	15	I		2	3			Experiencing one's existence via a role-play-type staging of one's personal drama Human-scale object inscribed in a dramatic threat/protection relation
MARTIN Bernhard	16	16	I		2				Creating morbid play through hybridization Human-scale object inscribed in a kinesthetic threat/protection relation
MARTIN Daria	23	8	I				4		Physically experiencing sensual pleasure Set centered around a live, personal action
MARTIN Jason	4	24	I				4		Understanding the mechanisms of perception through sensory experience Still, handcrafted image — painting type
MARTIN Kris	21	14	I				4	5	Experiencing the fragility of existence through its staging Human-scale, 'vestige of pop culture'-type object
MAYAUX Philippe	23	3	F						Physically experiencing sensual pleasure Contextual set that establishes a playful relationship with the visitor
MAZIÈRES Damien	15	2	F						Creating morbid play by shaping environments Contextual set that establishes a dreamlike relationship with the environment
MCCARTHY Paul	24	7	I	1	2	3			Physically experiencing trashy pleasure Set centered around a live, allegorical action
MCCOLLUM Allan	5	13	I	1					Understanding society and its codes in order to show their conditioning nature through mimesis Human-scale, 'vestige of the utopias'-type object
MCELHENY Josiah	3	13	I			3	4	5	Understanding the mechanisms of perception through format transposition Human-scale, 'vestige of the utopias'-type object
MCGEE Barry	9	5	I		2	3	4	5	Creating grotesque narratives using the parodic mode Set that associates an action with its remains-type traces
MCKENZIE Lucy	6	2	I			3	4	5	Understanding society and its codes in order to show their conditioning nature through derision Contextual set that establishes a dreamlike relationship with the environment
MCQUEEN Steve	20	7	I	1	2	3	4		Experiencing one's existence via a factual narrative of one's personal drama Set centered around a live, allegorical action
MECKSEPER Josephine	5	4	I					5	Understanding society and its codes in order to show their conditioning nature through mimesis Contextual set that establishes a hostile relationship with the visitor
MEESE Jonathan	17	8	I				4	5	Experiencing one's existence by creating a personal myth endowed with a metaphysical project Set centered around a live, personal action
MEHRETU Julie	2	23	I				4	5	Understanding the limits of our perception in terms of space Still, handcrafted image — drawing type
MELGAARD Bjarne	10	16	I		2	3		5	Creating grotesque narratives using the disquieting mode Human-scale object inscribed in a kinesthetic threat/protection relation
MERCIER Mathieu	13	14	F						Creating light-hearted play using marketing-type forms of communication Human-scale, 'vestige of pop culture'-type object
MIK Aernout	5	17	I			3	4	5	Understanding society and its codes in order to show their conditioning nature through mimesis Moving image with documentary-style mise-en-scene
MIKHAILOV Boris	21	22	I	1		3		5	Experiencing the fragility of existence through its staging Still image produced through the "visceral" use of an automated intermediary
MILLER John	19	14	I	1					Experiencing one's existence via a role-play-type staging of one's personal drama Human-scale, 'vestige of pop culture'-type object
MIRRA Helen	22	6	I				4	5	Experiencing the fragility of existence through auratic presentification Set that associates an action with its icon-type traces
MIYAJIMA Tatsuo	17	2	I	1	2				Experiencing one's existence by creating a personal myth endowed with a metaphysical project Contextual set that establishes a dreamlike relationship with the environment

Artist	MT	MN	SC	P1	P2	P3	P4	P5	Motors and Means
MOFFATT Tracey	8	22	I	1	2				Understanding society and its codes in order to denounce their unjust and exclusionary nature Still image produced through the "visceral" use of an automated intermediary
MOLINERO Anita	24	16	F						Physically experiencing trashy pleasure Human-scale object inscribed in a kinesthetic threat/protection relation
MONAHAN Matthew	16	13	I				4		Creating morbid play through hybridization Human-scale, 'vestige of the utopias'-type object
MONK Jonathan	20	3	I		2	3		5	Experiencing one's existence via a factual narrative of one's personal drama Contextual set that establishes a playful relationship with the visitor
MONTARON Laurent	12	6	F						Creating dreamlike narratives using the poetic mode Set that associates an action with its icon-type traces
MORI Mariko	17	10	I	1	2	3	4		Experiencing one's existence by creating a personal myth endowed with a metaphysical project Object sacralized by its technical character and directed towards the individual unconscious
MORIMURA Yasumasa	19	3	I	1	2	3	4		Experiencing one's existence via a role-play-type staging of one's personal drama Contextual set that establishes a playful relationship with the visitor
MORRIS Sarah	5	1	I	1	2	3	4	5	Understanding society and its codes in order to show their conditioning nature through mimesis Contextual set that establishes a clinical relationship with the environment
MORRISON Paul	22	15	I		2	3			Experiencing the fragility of existence through auratic presentification Human-scale object inscribed in a dramatic threat/protection relation
MOTI Melvin	22	13	I					5	Experiencing the fragility of existence through auratic presentification Human-scale, 'vestige of the utopias'-type object
MOUILLÉ Thierry	9	15	F						Creating grotesque narratives using the parodic mode Human-scale object inscribed in a dramatic threat/protection relation
MOULÈNE Jean-Luc	21	13	F						Experiencing the fragility of existence through its staging Human-scale, 'vestige of the utopias'-type object
MOULIN Nicolas	1	21	F						Understanding the limits of our perception in terms of time Still image produced through the "cold" use of an automated intermediary
MRÉJÈN Valérie	5	17	F						Understanding society and its codes in order to show their conditioning nature through mimesis Moving image with documentary-style mise-en-scene
MUECK Ron	22	10	I		2	3	4		Experiencing the fragility of existence through auratic presentification Object sacralized by its technical character and directed towards the individual unconscious
MULLER Dave	14	14	I	1			4		Creating light-hearted play through DIY-type work Human-scale, 'vestige of pop culture'-type object
MUNIZ Vik	14	6	I		2	3	4		Creating light-hearted play through DIY-type work Set that associates an action with its icon-type traces
MUÑOZ Juan	19	15	I	1	2				Experiencing one's existence via a role-play-type staging of one's personal drama Human-scale object inscribed in a dramatic threat/protection relation
MUNTEAN & ROSENBLUM	21	23	I		2	3	4		Experiencing the fragility of existence through its staging Still, handcrafted image — drawing type
MURAKAMI Takashi	13	9	I	1	2	3	4	5	Creating light-hearted play using marketing-type forms of communication Object sacralized by its technical character and directed towards the collective unconscious
MUTU Wangechi	16	23	I				4	5	Creating morbid play through hybridization Still, handcrafted image — drawing type
MYLAYNE Jean-Luc	21	21	IF					5	Experiencing the fragility of existence through its staging Still image produced through the "cold" use of an automated intermediary
NARA Yoshitomo	19	23	I		2	3	4		Experiencing one's existence via a role-play-type staging of one's personal drama Still, handcrafted image — drawing type
NASHASHIBI Rosalind	22	19	I				4		Experiencing the fragility of existence through auratic presentification Moving image conveying an introspective state through a slow tempo
NELSON Mike	5	13	I					5	Understanding society and its codes in order to show their conditioning nature through mimesis Human-scale, 'vestige of the utopias'-type object
NEPOMUCENO Maria	23	16	I					5	Physically experiencing sensual pleasure Human-scale object inscribed in a kinesthetic threat/protection relation
NESHAT Shirin	18	15	I	1	2	3	4	5	Experiencing one's existence by creating a socially engaged personal myth Human-scale object inscribed in a dramatic threat/protection relation
NETO Ernesto	23	16	I		2	3	4	5	Physically experiencing sensual pleasure Human-scale object inscribed in a kinesthetic threat/protection relation
NEUESCHWANDER Rivane	7	3	I		2	3	4	5	Understanding society and its codes in order to show their unjust and exclusionary nature through acts of sharing Contextual set that establishes a playful relationship with the visitor
NGUYEN-HATSUSHJBA Jun	8	6	I			3	4		Understanding society and its codes in order to denounce their unjust and exclusionary nature Set that associates an action with its icon-type traces

Artist	MT	MN	SC	P1	P2	P3	P4	P5	Motors and Means
NOBLE Paul	17	23	I				4		Experiencing one's existence by creating a personal myth endowed with a metaphysical project Still, handcrafted image — drawing type
NOBLE & WEBSTER	16	14	I			3	4		Creating morbid play through hybridization Human-scale, 'vestige of pop culture'-type object
NOLAND Cady	8	4	I	1					Understanding society and its codes in order to denounce their unjust and exclusionary nature Contextual set that establishes a hostile relationship with the visitor
NOONAN David	12	13	I				4	5	Creating dreamlike narratives using the poetic mode Human-scale, 'vestige of the utopias'-type object
NORDSTRÖM Jockum	12	23	I				4	5	Creating dreamlike narratives using the poetic mode Still, handcrafted image — drawing type
NOTELLET Olivier	12	3	F						Creating dreamlike narratives using the poetic mode Contextual set that establishes a playful relationship with the visitor
OCAMPO Manuel	9	24	I		2				Creating grotesque narratives using the parodic mode Still, handcrafted image — painting type
OEHLEN Albert	14	24	I	1		3			Creating light-hearted play through DIY-type work Still, handcrafted image — painting type
OFILI Chris	24	12	I				4		Physically experiencing trashy pleasure Object sacralized through a manual process, presenting a pagan dimension
ÖĞÜT Ahmet	20	3	I					5	Experiencing one's existence via a factual narrative of one's personal drama Contextual set that establishes a playful relationship with the visitor
OHANIAN Mélik	1	6	IF			3	4		Understanding the limits of our perception in terms of time Set that associates an action with its icon-type traces
OLOWSKA Paulina	12	13	I					5	Creating dreamlike narratives using the poetic mode Human-scale, 'vestige of the utopias'-type object
ONDÁK Roman	2	7	I				4	5	Understanding the limits of our perception in terms of space Set centered around a live, allegorical action
ONOFRE João	21	7	I		2	3			Experiencing the fragility of existence through its staging Set centered around a live, allegorical action
OP DE BEECK Hans	5	14	I			3	4		Understanding society and its codes in order to show their conditioning nature through mimesis Human-scale, 'vestige of pop culture'-type object
OPIE Julian	19	9	I	1	2	3	4		Experiencing one's existence via a role-play-type staging of one's personal drama Object sacralized by its technical character and directed towards the collective unconscious
OROZCO Gabriel	22	13	I	1	2	3	4	5	Experiencing the fragility of existence through auratic presentification Human-scale, 'vestige of the utopias'-type object
ORTEGA Damián	2	15	I			3	4	5	Understanding the limits of our perception in terms of space Human-scale object inscribed in a dramatic threat/protection relation
OTHONIEL Jean-Michel	22	12	IF	1		3		5	Experiencing the fragility of existence through auratic presentification Object sacralized through a manual process, presenting a pagan dimension
OWENS Laura	23	24	I			3	4	5	Physically experiencing sensual pleasure Still, handcrafted image — painting type
PACI Adrian	20	13	I			3	4	5	Experiencing one's existence via a factual narrative of one's personal drama Human-scale, 'vestige of the utopias'-type object
PANCHAL Gyan	21	11	F						Experiencing the fragility of existence through its staging Object sacralized through a manual process, presenting a metaphysical dimension
PARDO Jorge	2	1	I	1	2	3	4	5	Understanding the limits of our perception in terms of space Contextual set that establishes a clinical relationship with the environment
PARIS Guillaume	21	3	F						Experiencing the fragility of existence through its staging Contextual set that establishes a playful relationship with the visitor
PARKER Cornelia	3	12	I		2	3			Understanding the mechanisms of perception through format transposition Object sacralized through a manual process, presenting a pagan dimension
PARRENO Philippe	15	2	IF	1	2	3	4	5	Creating morbid play by shaping environments Contextual set that establishes a dreamlike relationship with the environment
PARRINO Steven	24	13	I	1	2				Physically experiencing trashy pleasure Human-scale, 'vestige of the utopias'-type object
PEINADO Bruno	13	14	F						Creating light-hearted play using marketing-type forms of communication Human-scale, 'vestige of pop culture'-type object
PENCHRÉAC'H Stéphane	24	24	F						Physically experiencing trashy pleasure Still, handcrafted image — painting type
PERIGOT Alexandre	6	3	F						Understanding society and its codes in order to show their conditioning nature through derision Contextual set that establishes a playful relationship with the visitor

Artist	MT	MN	SC	P1	P2	P3	P4	P5	Motors and Means
PERJOVSCHI Dan	8	3	I				4	5	Understanding society and its codes in order to denounce their unjust and exclusionary nature Contextual set that establishes a playful relationship with the visitor
PERNICE Manfred	5	13	I	1				5	Understanding society and its codes in order to show their conditioning nature through mimesis Human-scale, 'vestige of the utopias'-type object
PERRAMANT Bruno	3	24	F						Understanding the mechanisms of perception through format transposition Still, handcrafted image — painting type
PERRET Mai-Thu	15	13	I				4	5	Creating morbid play by shaping environments Human-scale, 'vestige of the utopias'-type object
PERROT Philippe	19	24	F						Experiencing one's existence via a role-play-type staging of one's personal drama Still, handcrafted image — painting type
PERRY Grayson	6	14	I				4		Understanding society and its codes in order to show their conditioning nature through derision Human-scale, 'vestige of pop culture'-type object
PETERMAN Dan	8	6	I		2				Understanding society and its codes in order to denounce their unjust and exclusionary nature Set that associates an action with its icon-type traces
PETITGAND Dominique	3	1	F						Understanding the mechanisms of perception through format transposition Contextual set that establishes a clinical relationship with the environment
PETTIBON Raymond	6	23	I	1	2	3	4	5	Understanding society and its codes in order to show their conditioning nature through derision Still, handcrafted image — drawing type
PEYTON Elizabeth	22	24	I	1	2	3	4	5	Experiencing the fragility of existence through auratic presentification Still, handcrafted image — painting type
PFEIFFER Paul	3	1	I		2	3	4	5	Understanding the mechanisms of perception through format transposition Contextual set that establishes a clinical relationship with the environment
PFLUMM Daniel	3	9	I				4		Understanding the mechanisms of perception through format transposition Object sacralized by its technical character and directed towards the collective unconscious
PHILIPSZ Susan	22	2	I				4	5	Experiencing the fragility of existence through auratic presentification Contextual set that establishes a dreamlike relationship with the environment
PHILLIPS Richard	3	24	I		2	3			Understanding the mechanisms of perception through format transposition Still, handcrafted image — painting type
PIENE Chloé	22	15	I		2	3			Experiencing the fragility of existence through auratic presentification Human-scale object inscribed in a dramatic threat/protection relation
PIERSON Jack	21	14	I	1	2		4	5	Experiencing the fragility of existence through its staging Human-scale, 'vestige of pop culture'-type object
PIFFARETTI Bernard	3	24	IF		2				Understanding the mechanisms of perception through format transposition Still, handcrafted image — painting type
PINAUD Pascal	3	5	F						Understanding the mechanisms of perception through format transposition Set that associates an action with its remains-type traces
PIPER Adrian	8	6	I	1					Understanding society and its codes in order to denounce their unjust and exclusionary nature Set that associates an action with its icon-type traces
PIPPIN Steven	3	1	I	1	2				Understanding the mechanisms of perception through format transposition Contextual set that establishes a clinical relationship with the environment
PITOISET Émilie	21	15	F						Experiencing the fragility of existence through its staging Human-scale object inscribed in a dramatic threat/protection relation
PITTMAN Lari	14	24	I	1					Creating light-hearted play through DIY-type work Still, handcrafted image — painting type
PIVI Paola	14	3	I				4		Creating light-hearted play through DIY-type work Contextual set that establishes a playful relationship with the visitor
PLENSA Jaume	22	2	I	1	2	3			Experiencing the fragility of existence through auratic presentification Contextual set that establishes a dreamlike relationship with the environment
PLESSEN Magnus	12	24	I		2	3	4		Creating dreamlike narratives using the poetic mode Still, handcrafted image — painting type
POITEVIN Éric	21	21	F						Experiencing the fragility of existence through its staging Still image produced through the "cold" use of an automated intermediary
PREGO Sergio	2	7	I			3			Understanding the limits of our perception in terms of space Set centered around a live, allegorical action
PRÉVIEUX Julien	6	6	F						Understanding society and its codes in order to show their conditioning nature through derision Set that associates an action with its icon-type traces
PRICE Seth	22	14	I					5	Experiencing the fragility of existence through auratic presentification Human-scale, 'vestige of pop culture'-type object
PRINA Stephen	6	1	I	1	2				Understanding society and its codes in order to show their conditioning nature through derision Contextual set that establishes a clinical relationship with the environment

Artist	MT	MN	SC	P1 P2 P3 P4 P5	Motors and Means
PRUITT Rob	14	14	I	2 5	Creating light-hearted play through DIY-type work Human-scale, 'vestige of pop culture'-type object
PUGNAIRE & RAFFINI	1	5	F		Understanding the limits of our perception in terms of time Set that associates an action with its remains-type traces
PURYEAR Martin	22	13	I	1	Experiencing the fragility of existence through auratic presentification Human-scale, 'vestige of the utopias'-type object
PUTRIH Tobias	2	13	I	4 5	Understanding the limits of our perception in terms of space Human-scale, 'vestige of the utopias'-type object
QIU ZHIJIE	17	8	I	5	Experiencing one's existence by creating a personal myth endowed with a metaphysical project Set centered around a live, personal action
QUAYTMAN R.H.	20	13	I	5	Experiencing one's existence via a factual narrative of one's personal drama Human-scale, 'vestige of the utopias'-type object
QUINN Marc	21	10	I	1 2 3 4 5	Experiencing the fragility of existence through its staging Object sacralized by its technical character and directed towards the individual unconscious
RAE Fiona	23	24	I	1	Physically experiencing sensual pleasure Still, handcrafted image — painting type
RAEDECKER Michael	22	13	I	3	Experiencing the fragility of existence through auratic presentification Human-scale, 'vestige of the utopias'-type object
RAMETTE Philippe	21	15	F		Experiencing the fragility of existence through its staging Human-scale object inscribed in a dramatic threat/protection relation
RAUCH Neo	11	24	I	2 3 4 5	Creating dreamlike narratives using the dramatic mode Still, handcrafted image — painting type
RAY Charles	22	10	I	1 4	Experiencing the fragility of existence through auratic presentification Object sacralized by its technical character and directed towards the individual unconscious
REHBERGER Tobias	2	1	I	1 2 3 4	Understanding the limits of our perception in terms of space Contextual set that establishes a clinical relationship with the environment
REYES Pedro	7	3	I	4 5	Understanding society and its codes in order to show their unjust and exclusionary nature through acts of sharing Contextual set that establishes a playful relationship with the visitor
REYLE Anselm	13	14	I	5	Creating light-hearted play using marketing-type forms of communication Human-scale, 'vestige of pop culture'-type object
REYNAUD-DEWAR Lili	10	12	F		Creating grotesque narratives using the disquieting mode Object sacralized through a manual process, presenting a pagan dimension
RHOADES Jason	13	4	I	1 2 3 4	Creating light-hearted play using marketing-type forms of communication Contextual set that establishes a hostile relationship with the visitor
RHODE Robin	14	8	I	4 5	Creating light-hearted play through DIY-type work Set centered around a live, personal action
RICHER Evariste	3	13	F		Understanding the mechanisms of perception through format transposition Human-scale, 'vestige of the utopias'-type object
RICHTER Daniel	11	24	I	3 4	Creating dreamlike narratives using the dramatic mode Still, handcrafted image — painting type
RIELLY James	22	24	I	2	Experiencing the fragility of existence through auratic presentification Still, handcrafted image — painting type
RIKA Noguchi	12	22	I	3	Creating dreamlike narratives using the poetic mode Still image produced through the "visceral" use of an automated intermediary
RIST Pipilotti	23	20	I	1 2 3 4 5	Physically experiencing sensual pleasure Moving image conveying an intoxicated state through a rapid tempo
ROCKENSCHAUB Gerwald	5	1	I	1	Understanding society and its codes in order to show their conditioning nature through mimesis Contextual set that establishes a clinical relationship with the environment
ROJAS Clare	12	14	I	4	Creating dreamlike narratives using the poetic mode Human-scale, 'vestige of pop culture'-type object
ROLLINS T. & K.O.S	7	13	I	1	Understanding society and its codes in order to show their unjust and exclusionary nature through acts of sharing Human-scale, 'vestige of the utopias'-type object
RONDINONE Ugo	15	15	I	2 3 4 5	Creating morbid play by shaping environments Human-scale object inscribed in a dramatic threat/protection relation
ROTH Daniel	12	12	I	2 3	Creating dreamlike narratives using the poetic mode Object sacralized through a manual process, presenting a pagan dimension
ROTHSCHILD Eva	22	10	I	4 5	Experiencing the fragility of existence through auratic presentification Object sacralized by its technical character and directed towards the individual unconscious
ROUSSEAU Samuel	16	14	F		Creating morbid play through hybridization Human-scale, 'vestige of pop culture'-type object

Artist	MT	MN	SC	P1 P2 P3 P4 P5	Motors and Means
RUBY Sterling	16	12	I	4	Creating morbid play through hybridization Object sacralized through a manual process, presenting a pagan dimension
RUFF Thomas	3	21	I	1 2 3	Understanding the mechanisms of perception through format transposition Still image produced through the "cold" use of an automated intermediary
RUILOVA Aïda	19	20	I	5	Experiencing one's existence via a role-play-type staging of one's personal drama Moving image conveying an intoxicated state through a rapid tempo
RUTAULT Claude	6	1	F		Understanding society and its codes in order to show their conditioning nature through derision Contextual set that establishes a clinical relationship with the environment
SACHS Tom	13	14	I	3 4	Creating light-hearted play using marketing-type forms of communication Human-scale, 'vestige of pop culture'-type object
SAILSTORFER Michael	14	15	I	5	Creating light-hearted play through DIY-type work Human-scale object inscribed in a dramatic threat/protection relation
SALA Anri	21	2	IF	2 3 4 5	Experiencing the fragility of existence through its staging Contextual set that establishes a dreamlike relationship with the environment
SALOMONE Yvan	17	5	F		Experiencing one's existence by creating a personal myth endowed with a metaphysical project Set that associates an action with its remains-type traces
SAMBA Chéri	18	24	I	1	Experiencing one's existence by creating a socially engaged personal myth Still, handcrafted image — painting type
SAMORE Sam	22	19	I	1 2	Experiencing the fragility of existence through auratic presentification Moving image conveying an introspective state through a slow tempo
SANDISON Charles	17	2	I	4 5	Experiencing one's existence by creating a personal myth endowed with a metaphysical project Contextual set that establishes a dreamlike relationship with the environment
SARACENO Tomàs	21	15	I	4 5	Experiencing the fragility of existence through its staging Human-scale object inscribed in a dramatic threat/protection relation
ŠARČEVIĆ Bojan	22	13	I	3	Experiencing the fragility of existence through auratic presentification Human-scale, 'vestige of the utopias'-type object
SARMENTO Julião	22	11	I	1 2	Experiencing the fragility of existence through auratic presentification Object sacralized through a manual process, presenting a metaphysical dimension
SASNAL Wilhelm	3	24	I	3 4 5	Understanding the mechanisms of perception through format transposition Still, handcrafted image — painting type
SAVILLE Jenny	24	24	I	3	Physically experiencing trashy pleasure Still, handcrafted image — painting type
SCANLAN Joe	14	14	I	2	Creating light-hearted play through DIY-type work Human-scale, 'vestige of pop culture'-type object
SCHEIBITZ Thomas	23	13	I	1 2 3 4 5	Physically experiencing sensual pleasure Human-scale, 'vestige of the utopias'-type object
SCHER Julia	5	4	I	1	Understanding society and its codes in order to show their conditioning nature through mimesis Contextual set that establishes a hostile relationship with the visitor
SCHINWALD Markus	15	15	I	2 4	Creating morbid play by shaping environments Human-scale object inscribed in a dramatic threat/protection relation
SCHNEIDER Anne-Marie	19	23	F		Experiencing one's existence via a role-play-type staging of one's personal drama Still, handcrafted image — drawing type
SCHNEIDER Gregor	24	4	I	2 3 4 5	Physically experiencing trashy pleasure Contextual set that establishes a hostile relationship with the visitor
SCHNITGER Lara	10	15	I	2 3	Creating grotesque narratives using the disquieting mode Human-scale object inscribed in a dramatic threat/protection relation
SCHULZE Andreas	10	3	I	1	Creating grotesque narratives using the disquieting mode Contextual set that establishes a playful relationship with the visitor
SCHÜTTE Thomas	16	12	I	1 2 3	Creating morbid play through hybridization Object sacralized through a manual process, presenting a pagan dimension
SCHUTZ Dana	24	24	I	5	Physically experiencing trashy pleasure Still, handcrafted image — painting type
SCURTI Franck	13	14	F		Creating light-hearted play using marketing-type forms of communication Human-scale, 'vestige of pop culture'-type object
SÉCHAS Alain	10	3	F		Creating grotesque narratives using the disquieting mode Contextual set that establishes a playful relationship with the visitor
ŠEDÁ Kateřina	20	5	I	5	Experiencing one's existence via a factual narrative of one's personal drama Set that associates an action with its remains-type traces
SEHGAL Tino	21	7	I	4 5	Experiencing the fragility of existence through its staging Set centered around a live, allegorical action

Artist	MT	MN	SC	P1 P2 P3 P4 P5	Motors and Means
SEKULA Allan	21	21	I	1	Experiencing the fragility of existence through its staging Still image produced through the "cold" use of an automated intermediary
SERRALONGUE Bruno	5	21	F		Understanding society and its codes in order to show their conditioning nature through mimesis Still image produced through the "cold" use of an automated intermediary
SERRANO Andres	24	21	I	1 2	Physically experiencing trashy pleasure Still image produced through the "cold" use of an automated intermediary
SHAW George	20	24	I	4	Experiencing one's existence via a factual narrative of one's personal drama Still, handcrafted image — painting type
SHAW Jim	19	2	I	2 3 5	Experiencing one's existence via a role-play-type staging of one's personal drama Contextual set that establishes a dreamlike relationship with the environment
SHAW Raqib	10	11	I	4 5	Creating grotesque narratives using the disquieting mode Object sacralized through a manual process, presenting a metaphysical dimension
SHEARER Steven	14	14	I	4 5	Creating light-hearted play through DIY-type work Human-scale, 'vestige of pop culture'-type object
SHONIBARE Yinka	8	15	I	2 3 4 5	Understanding society and its codes in order to denounce their unjust and exclusionary nature Human-scale object inscribed in a dramatic threat/protection relation
SHRIGLEY David	21	3	I	2 3 4 5	Experiencing the fragility of existence through its staging Contextual set that establishes a playful relationship with the visitor
SIBONY Gedi	2	13	I	4	Understanding the limits of our perception in terms of space Human-scale, 'vestige of the utopias'-type object
SIERRA Santiago	5	4	I	2 3 5	Understanding society and its codes in order to show their conditioning nature through mimesis Contextual set that establishes a hostile relationship with the visitor
SIGNER Roman	14	15	I	1	Creating light-hearted play through DIY-type work Human-scale object inscribed in a dramatic threat/protection relation
SIMON Taryn	8	21	I	3 4 5	Understanding society and its codes in order to denounce their unjust and exclusionary nature Still image produced through the "cold" use of an automated intermediary
SIMPSON Lorna	19	17	I	2 3	Experiencing one's existence via a role-play-type staging of one's personal drama Moving image with documentary-style mise-en-scene
SLOMINSKI Andreas	6	3	I	3	Understanding society and its codes in order to show their conditioning nature through derision Contextual set that establishes a playful relationship with the visitor
SMITH Josh	5	5	I	4 5	Understanding society and its codes in order to show their conditioning nature through mimesis Set that associates an action with its remains-type traces
SMITH Kiki	17	15	I	1 2	Experiencing one's existence by creating a personal myth endowed with a metaphysical project Human-scale object inscribed in a dramatic threat/protection relation
SNYDER Sean	5	6	I	5	Understanding society and its codes in order to show their conditioning nature through mimesis Set that associates an action with its icon-type traces
SOCIÉTÉ RÉALISTE	5	1	F		Understanding society and its codes in order to show their conditioning nature through mimesis Contextual set that establishes a clinical relationship with the environment
SOLAKOV Nedko	20	3	I	1	Experiencing one's existence via a factual narrative of one's personal drama Contextual set that establishes a playful relationship with the visitor
SOLOMOUKHA Kristina	14	3	F		Creating light-hearted play through DIY-type work Contextual set that establishes a playful relationship with the visitor
SONE Yutaka	21	12	I	3 4	Experiencing the fragility of existence through its staging Object sacralized through a manual process, presenting a pagan dimension
SORIN Pierrick	20	18	F		Experiencing one's existence via a factual narrative of one's personal drama Moving image with parodic mise-en-scene
SOSNOWSKA Monika	21	15	I	4 5	Experiencing the fragility of existence through its staging Human-scale object inscribed in a dramatic threat/protection relation
SPAULINGS Reena	5	5	I	4	Understanding society and its codes in order to show their conditioning nature through mimesis Set that associates an action with its remains-type traces
STARLING Simon	1	6	I	2 3 4 5	Understanding the limits of our perception in terms of time Set that associates an action with its icon-type traces
STARR Georgina	19	2	I	1	Experiencing one's existence via a role-play-type staging of one's personal drama Contextual set that establishes a dreamlike relationship with the environment
STEINBACH Haim	5	1	I	1	Understanding society and its codes in order to show their conditioning nature through mimesis Contextual set that establishes a clinical relationship with the environment
STERBAK Jana	17	11	I	1	Experiencing one's existence by creating a personal myth endowed with a metaphysical project Object sacralized through a manual process, presenting a metaphysical dimension
STEVENSON Michael	1	6	I	3 4	Understanding the limits of our perception in terms of time Set that associates an action with its icon-type traces

Artist	MT	MN	SC	P1	P2	P3	P4	P5	Motors and Means
STEWEN Dirk	22	13	I				4		Experiencing the fragility of existence through auratic presentification Human-scale, 'vestige of the utopias'-type object
STINGEL Rudolf	20	13	I			3	4		Experiencing one's existence via a factual narrative of one's personal drama Human-scale, 'vestige of the utopias'-type object
STOCKHOLDER Jessica	22	14	I	1	2	3	4		Experiencing the fragility of existence through auratic presentification Human-scale, 'vestige of pop culture'-type object
STOLL Georges Tony	20	6	F						Experiencing one's existence via a factual narrative of one's personal drama Set that associates an action with its icon-type traces
STRBA Annelies	12	19	I	1	2		4	5	Creating dreamlike narratives using the poetic mode Moving image conveying an introspective state through a slow tempo
STREULI Beat	22	21	I	1	2		4		Experiencing the fragility of existence through auratic presentification Still image produced through the "cold" use of an automated intermediary
STRUNZ Katja	1	13	I				4		Understanding the limits of our perception in terms of time Human-scale, 'vestige of the utopias'-type object
STRUTH Thomas	3	21	I	1	2				Understanding the mechanisms of perception through format transposition Still image produced through the "cold" use of an automated intermediary
SUGIMOTO Hiroshi	22	21	I	1	2				Experiencing the fragility of existence through auratic presentification Still image produced through the "cold" use of an automated intermediary
SUGITO Hiroshi	12	24	I			3	4	5	Creating dreamlike narratives using the poetic mode Still, handcrafted image — painting type
SUI-MEI TSE	1	2	I			3			Understanding the limits of our perception in terms of time Contextual set that establishes a dreamlike relationship with the environment
SULLIVAN Catherine	5	17	I			3	4	5	Understanding society and its codes in order to show their conditioning nature through mimesis Moving image with documentary-style mise-en-scene
SUPERFLEX	5	3	I				4	5	Understanding society and its codes in order to show their conditioning nature through mimesis Contextual set that establishes a playful relationship with the visitor
SZE Sarah	21	14	I				4	5	Experiencing the fragility of existence through its staging Human-scale, 'vestige of pop culture'-type object
TAAFFE Philip	22	24	I	1	2				Experiencing the fragility of existence through auratic presentification Still, handcrafted image — painting type
TAL R	12	14	I			3	4		Creating dreamlike narratives using the poetic mode Human-scale, 'vestige of pop culture'-type object
TALEC Nathalie	17	7	F						Experiencing one's existence by creating a personal myth endowed with a metaphysical project Set centered around a live, allegorical action
TAN Fiona	22	19	I		2	3	4		Experiencing the fragility of existence through auratic presentification Moving image conveying an introspective state through a slow tempo
TANDBERG Vibeke	19	17	I		2				Experiencing one's existence via a role-play-type staging of one's personal drama Moving image with documentary-style mise-en-scene
TATAH Djamel	20	24	F						Experiencing one's existence via a factual narrative of one's personal drama Still, handcrafted image — painting type
TAYLOR Al	2	5	I	1					Understanding the limits of our perception in terms of space Set that associates an action with its remains-type traces
TAYLOR-WOOD Sam	21	19	I	1	2	3	4		Experiencing the fragility of existence through its staging Moving image conveying an introspective state through a slow tempo
TELLER Juergen	21	22	I			3			Experiencing the fragility of existence through its staging Still image produced through the "visceral" use of an automated intermediary
TEMPLETON Ed	21	14	I			3			Experiencing the fragility of existence through its staging Human-scale, 'vestige of pop culture'-type object
THATER Diana	8	2	I	1	2	3	4	5	Understanding society and its codes in order to denounce their unjust and exclusionary nature Contextual set that establishes a dreamlike relationship with the environment
THAUBERGER Althea	21	17	I				4		Experiencing the fragility of existence through its staging Moving image with documentary-style mise-en-scene
THERRIEN Robert	14	15	I	1					Creating light-hearted play through DIY-type work Human-scale object inscribed in a dramatic threat/protection relation
THIDET Stéphane	22	16	F						Experiencing the fragility of existence through auratic presentification Human-scale object inscribed in a kinesthetic threat/protection relation
THOMAS Philippe	18	3	F						Experiencing one's existence by creating a socially engaged personal myth Contextual set that establishes a playful relationship with the visitor
THURNAUER Agnès	18	14	F						Experiencing one's existence by creating a socially engaged personal myth Human-scale, 'vestige of pop culture'-type object

Artist	MT	MN	SC	P1 P2 P3 P4 P5	Motors and Means
TICHY Jan	22	2	I	5	Experiencing the fragility of existence through auratic presentification Contextual set that establishes a dreamlike relationship with the environment
TILLMANS Wolfgang	22	22	I	1 2 3 4 5	Experiencing the fragility of existence through auratic presentification Still image produced through the "visceral" use of an automated intermediary
TIRAVANIJA Rirkrit	7	7	IF	1 2 3 4 5	Understanding society and its codes in order to show their unjust and exclusionary nature through acts of sharing Set centered around a live, allegorical action
TIXADOR & POINCHEVAL	12	13	F		Creating dreamlike narratives using the poetic mode Human-scale, 'vestige of the utopias'-type object
TOBIAS Gert & Uwe	12	12	I	4	Creating dreamlike narratives using the poetic mode Object sacralized through a manual process, presenting a pagan dimension
TODERI Grazia	11	19	I	2	Creating dreamlike narratives using the dramatic mode Moving image conveying an introspective state through a slow tempo
TOGUO Barthélémy	8	16	I	2	Understanding society and its codes in order to denounce their unjust and exclusionary nature Human-scale object inscribed in a kinesthetic threat/protection relation
TOMASELLI Fred	12	23	I	3	Creating dreamlike narratives using the poetic mode Still, handcrafted image — drawing type
TOSANI Patrick	22	21	I	1	Experiencing the fragility of existence through auratic presentification Still image produced through the "cold" use of an automated intermediary
TRECARTIN Ryan	16	14	I	5	Creating morbid play through hybridization Human-scale, 'vestige of pop culture'-type object
TROCKEL Rosemarie	6	13	I	1 2	Understanding society and its codes in order to show their conditioning nature through derision Human-scale, 'vestige of the utopias'-type object
TROUVÉ Tatiana	15	13	IF	5	Creating morbid play by shaping environments Human-scale, 'vestige of the utopias'-type object
TSCHÄPE Janaina	23	24	I	3 4 5	Physically experiencing sensual pleasure Still, handcrafted image — painting type
TUAZON Oscar	2	13	I	5	Understanding the limits of our perception in terms of space Human-scale, 'vestige of the utopias'-type object
TURK Gavin	6	3	I	5	Understanding society and its codes in order to show their conditioning nature through derision Contextual set that establishes a playful relationship with the visitor
TURSIC & MILLE	3	24	F		Understanding the mechanisms of perception through format transposition Still, handcrafted image — painting type
TUYMANS Luc	22	24	I	1 2 3 4 5	Experiencing the fragility of existence through auratic presentification Still, handcrafted image — painting type
TYKKÄ Salla	22	19	I	2 3 4	Experiencing the fragility of existence through auratic presentification Moving image conveying an introspective state through a slow tempo
TYSON Keith	9	14	I	3 4	Creating grotesque narratives using the parodic mode Human-scale, 'vestige of pop culture'-type object
TYSON Nicola	24	24	I	1	Physically experiencing trashy pleasure Still, handcrafted image — painting type
UGLOW Alan	22	13	I	1	Experiencing the fragility of existence through auratic presentification Human-scale, 'vestige of the utopias'-type object
UKLANSKI Piotr	3	3	I	2 3	Understanding the mechanisms of perception through format transposition Contextual set that establishes a playful relationship with the visitor
VAN DER WERVE Guido	19	6	I	5	Experiencing one's existence via a role-play-type staging of one's personal drama Set that associates an action with its icon-type traces
VAN LAMSWEERDE Inez	23	22	I	1	Physically experiencing sensual pleasure Still image produced through the "visceral" use of an automated intermediary
VAREJÃO Adriana	16	16	I	2 3 4	Creating morbid play through hybridization Human-scale object inscribed in a kinesthetic threat/protection relation
VEILHAN Xavier	3	9	IF	1 2	Understanding the mechanisms of perception through format transposition Object sacralized by its technical character and directed towards the collective unconscious
VERNA Jean-Luc	16	23	F		Creating morbid play through hybridization Still, handcrafted image — drawing type
VEZZOLI Francesco	5	18	I	3 4 5	Understanding society and its codes in order to show their conditioning nature through mimesis Moving image with parodic mise-en-scene
VIOLETTE Banks	15	14	I	4 5	Creating morbid play by shaping environments Human-scale, 'vestige of pop culture'-type object
VO Danh	18	13	I	5	Experiencing one's existence by creating a socially engaged personal myth Human-scale, 'vestige of the utopias'-type object

Artist	MT	MN	SC	P1	P2	P3	P4	P5	Motors and Means
VON BONIN Cosima	7	2	I				4	5	Understanding society and its codes in order to show their unjust and exclusionary nature through acts of sharing Contextual set that establishes a dreamlike relationship with the environment
VON BRANDENBURG Ulla	12	13	IF					5	Creating dreamlike narratives using the poetic mode Human-scale, 'vestige of the utopias'-type object
VONNA MICHELL Tris	1	8	I					5	Understanding the limits of our perception in terms of time Set centered around a live, personal action
WALKER Kara	8	2	I		2	3	4	5	Understanding society and its codes in order to denounce their unjust and exclusionary nature Contextual set that establishes a dreamlike relationship with the environment
WALKER Kelley	5	14	I				4	5	Understanding society and its codes in order to show their conditioning nature through mimesis Human-scale, 'vestige of pop culture'-type object
WALL Jeff	21	21	I	1	2	3			Experiencing the fragility of existence through its staging Still image produced through the "cold" use of an automated intermediary
WANG DU	5	14	IF		2		4		Understanding society and its codes in order to show their conditioning nature through mimesis Human-scale, 'vestige of pop culture'-type object
WARDILL Emily	19	15	I					5	Experiencing one's existence via a role-play-type staging of one's personal drama Human-scale object inscribed in a dramatic threat/protection relation
WEARING Gillian	19	17	I	1	2	3	4		Experiencing one's existence via a role-play-type staging of one's personal drama Moving image with documentary-style mise-en-scene
WEBER Marnie	10	3	I					5	Creating grotesque narratives using the disquieting mode Contextual set that establishes a playful relationship with the visitor
WEERASETHAKUL Apichatpong	7	7	I					5	Understanding society and its codes in order to show their unjust and exclusionary nature through acts of sharing Set centered around a live, allegorical action
WEINSTEIN Matthew	15	14	I			3			Creating morbid play by shaping environments Human-scale, 'vestige of pop culture'-type object
WEKUA Andro	12	2	I				4	5	Creating dreamlike narratives using the poetic mode Contextual set that establishes a dreamlike relationship with the environment
WELLING James	3	21	I	1					Understanding the mechanisms of perception through format transposition Still image produced through the "cold" use of an automated intermediary
WERMERS Nicole	2	13	I				4		Understanding the limits of our perception in terms of space Human-scale, 'vestige of the utopias'-type object
WEST Franz	6	16	I	1					Understanding society and its codes in order to show their conditioning nature through derision Human-scale object inscribed in a kinesthetic threat/protection relation
WHITE Pae	14	12	I				4		Creating light-hearted play through DIY-type work Object sacralized through a manual process, presenting a pagan dimension
WHITEREAD Rachel	22	13	I	1	2	3	4	5	Experiencing the fragility of existence through auratic presentification Human-scale, 'vestige of the utopias'-type object
WILCOX T. J.	3	14	I	1	2	3	4		Understanding the mechanisms of perception through format transposition Human-scale, 'vestige of pop culture'-type object
WILEY Kehinde	18	24	I					5	Experiencing one's existence by creating a socially engaged personal myth Still, handcrafted image — painting type
WILKES Cathy	16	14	I					5	Creating morbid play through hybridization Human-scale, 'vestige of pop culture'-type object
WILLIAMS Christopher	3	21	I	1	2				Understanding the mechanisms of perception through format transposition Still image produced through the "cold" use of an automated intermediary
WILLIAMS Sue	23	24	I	1	2	3			Physically experiencing sensual pleasure Still, handcrafted image — painting type
WILSON Jane & Louise	8	17	I		2	3	4	5	Understanding society and its codes in order to denounce their unjust and exclusionary nature Moving image with documentary-style mise-en-scene
WOHNSEIFER Johannes	6	4	I			3			Understanding society and its codes in order to show their conditioning nature through derision Contextual set that establishes a hostile relationship with the visitor
WOLFSON Jordan	1	14	I				4		Understanding the limits of our perception in terms of time Human-scale, 'vestige of pop culture'-type object
WOOL Christopher	22	14	I	1	2	3	4	5	Experiencing the fragility of existence through auratic presentification Human-scale, 'vestige of pop culture'-type object
WRIGHT Richard	22	2	I		2	3	4		Experiencing the fragility of existence through auratic presentification Contextual set that establishes a dreamlike relationship with the environment
WURM Erwin	21	3	I		2	3	4	5	Experiencing the fragility of existence through its staging Contextual set that establishes a playful relationship with the visitor
WYN EVANS Cerith	3	2	I	1	2	3			Understanding the mechanisms of perception through format transposition Contextual set that establishes a dreamlike relationship with the environment

Artist	MT	MN	SC	P1 P2 P3 P4 P5	Motors and Means
X BALL Barry	16	15	I	1	Creating morbid play through hybridization Human-scale object inscribed in a dramatic threat/protection relation
XHAFA Sislej	6	15	I	3 4 5	Understanding society and its codes in order to show their conditioning nature through derision Human-scale object inscribed in a dramatic threat/protection relation
XU BING	7	6	I	1	Understanding society and its codes in order to show their unjust and exclusionary nature through acts of sharing Set that associates an action with its icon-type traces
XU ZHEN (MADEIN)	5	3	I	5	Understanding society and its codes in order to show their conditioning nature through mimesis Contextual set that establishes a playful relationship with the visitor
YAN LEI	19	24	I	4	Experiencing one's existence via a role-play-type staging of one's personal drama Still, handcrafted image — painting type
YAN PEI-MING	22	24	IF	4 5	Experiencing the fragility of existence through auratic presentification Still, handcrafted image — painting type
YANG FUDONG	12	19	I	3 4 5	Creating dreamlike narratives using the poetic mode Moving image conveying an introspective state through a slow tempo
YANG Haegue	21	13	I	5	Experiencing the fragility of existence through its staging Human-scale, 'vestige of the utopias'-type object
YASS Catherine	2	2	I	4	Understanding the limits of our perception in terms of space Contextual set that establishes a dreamlike relationship with the environment
YASSEF Virginie	9	14	F		Creating grotesque narratives using the parodic mode Human-scale, 'vestige of pop culture'-type object
YUSKAVAGE Lisa	23	24	I	5	Physically experiencing sensual pleasure Still, handcrafted image — painting type
ZARKA Raphaël	3	13	F		Understanding the mechanisms of perception through format transposition Human-scale, 'vestige of the utopias'-type object
ZHANG ENLI	22	14	I	5	Experiencing the fragility of existence through auratic presentification Human-scale, 'vestige of pop culture'-type object
ZHANG XIAOGANG	22	24	I	4 5	Experiencing the fragility of existence through auratic presentification Still, handcrafted image — painting type
ZIMMERMAN Peter	4	24	I	4	Understanding the mechanisms of perception through sensory experience Still, handcrafted image — painting type
ZIPP Thomas	15	15	I	4	Creating morbid play by shaping environments Human-scale object inscribed in a dramatic threat/protection relation
ZITTEL Andrea	5	4	I	1 2 3 4 5	Understanding society and its codes in order to show their conditioning nature through mimesis Contextual set that establishes a hostile relationship with the visitor
ZMIJEWSKI Artur	5	17	I	3 4 5	Understanding society and its codes in order to show their conditioning nature through mimesis Moving image with documentary-style mise-en-scene
ZOBERNIG Heimo	5	1	I	1	Understanding society and its codes in order to show their conditioning nature through mimesis Contextual set that establishes a clinical relationship with the environment

Translated and extended from the 2011 French original
*600 **démarches d'artistes***

Translator: Anna Preger

éditions jannink

127 rue de la Glacière

75013 Paris

www.editions-jannink.com

Distribution

Les Presses du réel

35 rue Colson

21000 Dijon

www.lespressesdureel.com

No. ISBN 978-2-916067-88-9

Printed in August 2013

by Imprimerie Stipa